MY CHAPLIN

Drawn by Satyajit Ray [1921–1992], the legendary Indian filmmaker, in 1953, as a part of cover design of a book in Bengali—*Charlie Chaplin*—by Mrinal Sen

MY CHAPLIN

MRINAL SEN

NEW AGE

REGD OFFICE
New Age Publishers (P) Ltd
8/1 Chintamoni Das Lane, Kolkata 700 009, India
ncbapvtltd@eth.net

OVERSEAS
NCBA (UK) Ltd, 149 Park Avenue North, Northampton, NN3 2HY, UK
ncbauk@yahoo.com

EXPORT
NCBA Exports Pvt. Ltd, 212 Shahpur Jat, New Delhi 110 049
ncbaexports@ncbaindia.com

BRANCHES

212 Shahpur Jat
New Delhi 110 049
ncbadel@ncbapvtltd.com

House No. 3-1-315, 1st Floor
Nimboliadda, Kachiguda, Hyderabad 500 027
ncbahydb@ncbapvtltd.com

Shop Nos. 3 & 4, Vinayak Towers
681/B Budhwar Peth
Appa Balwant Chowk, Pune 411 002
ncbapune@ncbapvtltd.com

GSS Shopping Complex, 1st Floor
Opposite College Post Office,
Convent Road, Ernakulam 682 035
ncbaernk@ncbapvtltd.com

Shop No. 15, Bharati Towers,
Ground Floor, Forest Park,
Bhubaneswar 751 001
ncbabub@ncbapvtltd.com

Radhamayee Complex (Second Floor)
Opp. SBI, Panbazar, Jaswanta Road
Guwahati 781 001
ncbaguwahati@ncbapvtltd.com

My Chaplin *by* Mrinal Sen

PUBLISHER
New Age Publishers (P) Ltd
8/1 Chintamoni Das Lane, Kolkata 700 009, India

PRINTER
New Central Book Agency (P) Ltd
Web-Offset Division, Dhulagarh, Sankrail, Howrah

First Edition: 2013

COVER & BOOK DESIGN: Soumen Paul

FRONT COVER PHOTO:
Chaplin in 1966, conducting the music for *A Countess from Hong Kong*

BACK COVER PHOTO: Author

ISBN 978 81 7819 110 2

Price: ₹ 375.00

IN MEMORY OF

KK Mahajan

my cameraman [1969 – 1989], who died of cancer.
When he looked through my camera for the first time—and that was his first feature film—I asked him to remember the quote from Niels Bohr, the iconic physicist: Confidence comes from not only being always right, but also from not fearing to be wrong.
KK is dead, I am still alive.

KK with his three-year-old daughter Tanya

Acknowledgements

Since this book is about *my* Chaplin, who may or may not be the Chaplin of others, I freely state that all quotes used by me in the text are approximations rendered in my own words.

I gratefully acknowledge some invaluable books which have been part of my writing of this one. They include David Robinson's *Chaplin: His Life and Art*, presented to me at Cannes 1986 with his personal note: 'For Mrinal, with affection, admiration and gratitude for the great films you have given us and will continue to give us. David Robinson, May 1986'. Others are Robert Payne's *The Great God Pan*, Jay Leyda's *Kino: A History of the Russian and Soviet Film*, Theodore Huff's *Charlie Chaplin*, Chaplin's *My Autobiography*, and my own *Always Being Born*.

I am also grateful to the following newspapers which have featured many of my pieces on Chaplin over the years—*The Statesman, The Times of India, Ananda Bazar Patrika, Aaj Kaal,* and several other periodicals and publications.

My gratitude to my editor Anjum Katyal for entering into the spirit of this book as much as for the changes that she suggested in the text, and also for her careful reading of various drafts of the manuscript; not to speak of Subas Maitra who, while checking the proof, did an extraordinary job of further brushing the text. As typesetters of the book, Soumi Biswas and Swapan Sarkar, too, did, respectively, magnificent job. Since the text is stuffed with intricacies at various levels, Surya Kanto Chakraborty did an impressive job of Indexing. Last but not the least, Amitabha Sen, the Director of New Age and the major driving force behind this publication, and Soumen Paul, the Production Head and designer of the book, left no stone unturned to turn my ideas into reality. Amitabha, as a publisher, will always be remembered for his stupendous generosity and literary verve.

Mrinal Sen

The Great Dictator

' ... You are men! You have the love of humanity
in your heart. Soldiers! Do not fight for slavery.
Fight for liberty. You, the people, have the power,
the power to create machines, the power to create
happiness. You people have the power
to make this life free and beautiful,
to make this life a wonderful adventure ... '

CHARLIE CHAPLIN

CONTENTS

1

An overview

A glorious concept—the concept of an average man.

The little tramp.

He sees the millionaire throw away a burning cigarette. He picks it up as though it is his own. He places it between his lips, takes a puff, lets out a cloud of smoke and puts on an air of almost philosophical detachment. Splendid. Simple. Serious. Forthright.

PEOPLE LAUGH.

He walks and walks a long way and continues to build stories, one after another, on and on. He walks through history and becomes history. Through diverse 'adventures' he laughs at himself. He also pities himself a little. He tries to meet the world head-on, to put on a brave face.

PEOPLE LAUGH AND THINK.

He climbs into the dug-out and hides in the trenches to fight the enemy in the First Great War. Undaunted by the cold and the rain he takes advantage of volleys of bullets fired fiercely from a vantage position. He raises a bottle in a firm grip. A bullet hits the bottlecap and the bottle opens. He drinks deeply. And then lifts his cigarette to light it with the help of further fire. He applies his inimitable tricks to outsmart his enemies and finally to arrest the Kaiser, all with perfect elan. Instantly a line appears on the screen: 'And peace to the world!'

PEOPLE LAUGH AND THINK AND GROW.

Time flies, films fill the cans. He continues to remain a little man, a clown, infinitely resourceful yet bewildered by a world that has no place for him. He looks around and stands before the mirror. He confronts his double. The double stands for untold evil. He paces back and forth and comes to realise that the world is sliding into crisis. The history of the world takes a turn, hopes and beliefs are belied, everything is topsy-turvy. He stands between the two Wars, the Great Wars, the First and the Second. He knows what is what, knows that he will no more be quite so nice, that the people who have liked him vaguely will have to make up their minds. Now he and his double appear on the scene.

PEOPLE LAUGH AND THINK AND GROW AND JUDGE.

They poke fun at the double.

Change—as Hitler

Instead of clouds lifting and the sun breaking through, the darkness deepens. He arrives at a critical juncture of an epoch, stops awhile, grows desperate, and throws a challenge at everything that comes his way. He tosses away his bowler hat, flings off his buttoned coat, trims his moustache. Yet his persona remains largely unchanged, his manners are more or less the same. He grabs the job of a clerk in a metropolitan bank in France. When the stock exchange is in panic and Depression years in the offing, he receives, with his pay packet, a notice of dismissal. In the lean years that follow, when millionaires face bad times, he floats a business of his own. Regardless of age, he indiscriminately plays lover to an assortment of wealthy women. It is a sport with fatal consequences for other players because he begins to kill off these women, one by one, and steal their wealth. Dreadful! Amazing!! Hilarious!!!

PEOPLE LAUGH AND THINK AND WONDER WHAT IT IS ALL ABOUT.

Investigators charge the dismissed bank clerk with mass murder—the murder of twelve women. He is condemned to death. Keeping cool he says, in no-

nonsense manner: 'One murder makes a villain, millions a hero. Numbers sanctify.'

Mass-murder! He declares that murder is the logical extension of business. And he concludes: 'All business is ruthless business'.

PEOPLE, NOT ALL, SIT UP AND TAKE NOTICE.

Portrait of Chaplin in the 60s

Shakespeare said that genius is to madness alike. Chaplin seems to have asserted that 'ruthlessness is to comicality alike'. Putting together the two extremes of ruthlessness and comicality, Chaplin provided a unique example of incredibly creative originality transcending all conceivable absurdities and yet projecting supreme wisdom, the like of which the world of cinema has never seen.

When Jean Renoir [1894 – 1979], the French master, was asked to name three directors whom he considered the best filmmakers, he allegedly counted on his fingers: 'Charlot, Charlot, and Charlot' (Charlie, Charlie, and Charlie).

He and the kid behind the wall

ALF. REEVES
Presents
Karno's London
Comedians
IN THE BIG GRIEF-
DESTROYING FARCE

A NIGHT IN A LONDO[N]
SECRET SOCIE[TY]

PRESENTING THAT CLEVER ENGLISH COMEDIAN—

CHARLES CHAPLIN

YOU'LL LAUGH, YOU'LL SMILE, YOU'LL YELL AND YOU'LL SCREAM

THE WOW-WOWS

BIELE & GIRARD

THE YANKEE AND THE SWEDE

The Daintiest Instrumentalist in Vaudeville

INEZ LAWSON

TRUMPET SOLOIST

THE GENTEEL SINGING

OH! YOU'LL REMEMBER ME

2

'Chapman, Caplin or something ...'

"Ask me where I have been,
And I'll tell you: 'Things keep on happening'"
(Pablo Neruda, *Residence on Earth*)

Happenings! Happenings all day long. All the time. And it was same with Charles Chaplin—'happenings' all the time. Being an incorruptible Indian and a Chaplin-addict I, for one, shall pick from his truckload of 'happenings' just two events; just two that took place during his world tour in 1931—one in the third week of September and the other three weeks earlier.

September 1931. In his own country Mahatma Gandhi, India's moral and political leader, lived a modest life, as an ascetic, so to say, bare-bodied, and dressed in a white loincloth, a rough blanket thrown over his shoulder when strictly necessary. As for his footwear, he wore just a pair of sandals, no socks. Being a father figure, he was affectionately called *Bapu* (father) by all. He came to London in September 1931, on the official invitation of the British Government headed by Ramsay MacDonald [1866–1937], to participate in the Second Round Table Conference. He never lived in a plush hotel—in India or anywhere else. In London he lived in the East End—as he described it, 'among the poor'—at Kingsley Hall, a simple community centre set up by the Christian pacifist sisters, Muriel and Doris Lister, not far from Bow Road. He did not have a problem living a spartan life in a tiny cell measuring just a few square feet. He slept on a mat on the floor and always kept his door open.

Charlie Chaplin, then on a world tour, was in London at the time. Having become a silent movie star in Hollywood, Chaplin, following his itinerary, came to London primarily for the British premiere of *City Lights* at the Dominion Theatre; but being in London after years, also to be 'emotionally stimulated'. Besides making films and presenting them, which kept him busy, he had a flood of thoughts popping into his head and he wanted to share them with 'great people' of diverse disciplines. With the Depression taking its toll on the European economy, Chaplin, himself a distressed man, felt the urge to discuss matters with George Bernard Shaw, H. G. Wells, Winston Churchill, Lloyd George and also with Einstein, Pablo Picasso, Thomas Mann and several others. Now, he wanted to meet Gandhi.

Muriel Lister and her sister, who ran Kingsley Hall, did their best to keep records about Gandhi. Muriel struggled to keep the press at bay, and organised many public and private meetings about religion and politics. She put in writing the relationship Gandhi had developed with the local people. The book subtly brought out the parallel position of the working classes of London and the Mahatma's own countrymen.

One of Muriel Lister's clearest mental images was that of the Mahatma sitting with a telegram in his hand, looking distinctly confused. Grouped around him were his own people, awaiting his response. As Muriel walked in, she heard a disapproving voice saying: '... but he is only a buffoon, there is no point in going to meet him.' The telegram was handed over for refusal when she saw who it was from.

'But don't you know the name, Bapu?' she asked, intrigued.

'No,' he said unassumingly.

'Charlie Chaplin! He is the world's hero. You simply must meet him. His art is rooted in the life of the working people. He understands the poor people as much as you do. He always honours them in his pictures.'

Eventually they met. The meeting was in September 1931. The opportunity came when Gandhi was visiting a doctor friend (Dr Katiyal) not far from Kingsley Hall in the East End. Crowds had gathered to follow Gandhi and even more crowds to see Chaplin. Quite a number even clambered over the garden fence to look through the windows of the house. It was only a brief meeting, but it made the front pages of the newspapers together with a delightful cartoon published in a daily, titled 'When two great prophets meet!'

Gandhi did not have time to spare. So Chaplin said whatever he had to in a rush, almost in a single breath. Initially Gandhi could not figure out how to reply. On Chaplin's insistence he answered a few

'When two great prophets meet!'

questions. His replies were rather brief but he never failed to be gracious. At times he made himself quite clear, however unclear he might have appeared to Chaplin. Regarding the Oriental lifestyle and the economy he said that in the Indian situation he was opposed to machinery. As far as their clothes were concerned, he said that instead of machinery leading to overproduction he would prefer *charka* (hand-wheel) and handloom. Besides, he could not agree with Chaplin on many other issues because most of his views, he thought, were obtrusively Occidental. However, he was very polite and invited his visitor to watch him and his colleagues at prayers because it was time. Offering no apology he said, 'Sorry, there is no room for you. You had better sit on the sofa and we shall sit on the floor.' Later, Chaplin wrote, 'Gandhi and his men did not feel embarrassed to sit on the floor in front of me but I felt awkward sitting on the sofa and literally looking down on him and his colleagues.' Chaplin was deeply impressed, and noted: '... a realistic, virile-minded visionary with a will of iron ... A tremendous personality.'

Bernard Shaw [1856–1950] in a letter to his friend Lady Nancy Astor [1879–1964], the first woman MP to sit in the House of Commons, said, 'Mahatma Gandhi is a saint under the covenant of grace.'

Earlier, Chaplin was flanked by the same two

persons—Bernard Shaw and Lady Nancy Astor—in the packed Dominion Theatre at the premiere of *City Lights*. Outside the theatre, a crowd of people stood in the pouring rain to catch a glimpse of, in particular, Chaplin. Being a showman in the presence of such an august personality, Chaplin was somewhat nervous about Shaw's reaction to the film. Shaw, however, liked the film very much, and laughed and cried along with the others. Later, a reporter asked Shaw what he thought of the idea of Chaplin playing Hamlet. 'Why not?' Shaw replied. He added, 'Long before Mr Chaplin became famous, and had got no further than throwing bricks or having them thrown at him, I was struck with his haunting, tragic expression, remarkably like Henry Irving's [1838–1905] (the greatest actor of British Stage in those days), and Irving made a tremendous success as Hamlet—or rather of an invention of his own which he called Hamlet.' A great compliment, indeed, coming from GBS, a highly accomplished theatre critic!

That was how the man was shaped—Charles Spencer Chaplin. That was how he was known all over the world. That was how he gained millions of admirers, although, to use his own words, 'I made a few enemies in America—that is all.'

Chaplin's childhood was bleak, staggeringly bleak. Plenty of apocryphal anecdotes about his childhood were later rolled into circulation, manufactured, by and large, by the writers, and, quite understandably, when the Un-American Activities diatribe was at its peak, by the Federal Bureau of Investigation (FBI) in the United States. Even the British MI5 said that there was no conclusive document to establish his exact birthplace. Furthermore, in the locked drawer of a bureau left behind after Chaplin's death, his family found a letter from a man in England named Jack Hill, according to whom Chaplin was born in a caravan that belonged to the Gypsy Queen, 'who was my aunty'. With his characteristic humour Chaplin reportedly conjectured that the idea of such a mystery surrounding his birth was quite delicious.

But to cut a long story short, and not allow the chaotic situation to grow out of hand, it could as well be assumed that Chaplin was born on 16 April 1889 (by an odd coincidence, the same year as Hitler!) in a slum somewhere in the south of London, not in South Africa (!) or anywhere else. They were a family of four—he, his stepbrother, four years older, and their parents.

His father was a popular music hall comedian, singing, dancing and performing novelty acts, not really with much refinement or sophistication. Nevertheless, he was loved by the music hall audiences. His mother was also a comedienne at the same theatre, but she kept indifferent health. Thus, although his father was quite regular at his job, his mother was not, due to illness. Ever so often she had to be hospitalised and even sent to the mental asylum or infirmary, and all this resulted in a reduction of income. So the family suffered from acute financial and security anxieties.

The two brothers—Sydney and Charlie—had very little formal education. Sydney, at a young age, worked hard moving from one workhouse to another and barely managed to earn his keep. Charlie's preference was to sing and dance in the streets and parks, and pick up some money busking. All in all, the family had a tough life. On top of this, his father squandered precious money on drink. He died, aged only thirty-seven, reducing the family to three—Sydney, Charlie and the sick mother. His mother turned to taking in stitching at home, bringing in a pittance, while Sydney joined the ships, hopping from one ship to another, and earning a bit more. Chaplin was then his mother's sole companion.

Quite often the mother and the son would sit by the window watching the people passing by along the street. With nothing else to do, watching was a plausible pastime. What did the mother and the son watch? People walking fast? Flurried, bustling? Styles of walking? The mother would pick out a funny one and imitate him, and the son would laugh hugely. Or she would select another, quite tall, and start walking on tiptoes. The son would do likewise, both of them giggling madly. They would see a child slip down from his mother's clasp and crawl through the dense crowd—an intriguing and frightening sight for them both. The streets and lanes were filled with ordinary men and women who lived lives of struggle and squalour, whom the mother and the son observed through their window. That was the life they led, filled with both love and pain.

The mother and the son were never tired of being on the watch, enjoying every minute of the 'happenings' outside the window. Most importantly, what the son did was to study his mother miming. The mother miming and the son learning and laughing. He was charmed by his mother's ability to caricature. Later, when Chaplin came of age, he said about her, 'She was the most outstanding mimic I ever saw.'

The mother and the son, just the two of them together, building a world of their own in which, willy-nilly, the mother was the teacher and the son the pupil. Both looking outside into the world—from the world they built and lived in and loved. And the son turned out to be the world's most renowned mimic, with no one to equal him. This he candidly admitted in his autobiography: 'In the art of pantomime, without false modesty, I am a master.' Albert Einstein, the great scientist, at the end of a private debate about the years of Depression, said about him, 'Who said you are a comedian? You are an economist!'

A note on the mother: When she was in her early 60s, Hannah Chaplin died at Glendale Hospital,

California. While she was in hospital, Chaplin visited his mother every day, and forced himself to laugh and joke with her. The day before she died the nurses at the hospital heard them laughing together. Soon after, she slipped into a coma. She died on 28 August 1928. This Londoner-cum-comedienne, born and raised in a filthy slum, was buried in the Hollywood Cemetery.

Back to the fledgling performer, Charles. From 1910–1913 he formed part of a troupe, headed by a well-known music hall owner, Fred Karno, that made a long trip to America. There was not

Mother Hannah Chaplin

Hannah's grave in the Hollywood Cemetery

much of difference between the English music hall and America's vaudeville, but the competition was tough and the American audience seemed to like vaudeville much more than the English counterpart. Undaunted, Fred Karno's team continued with their shows, travelling extensively with the entire group in the hope that the company would ultimately succeed. If not the team in its totality, a young man, hardly seventeen, gave a good enough account of himself for Mack Sennett of Keystone Film Company to enquire about him. He lost no time in rushing a telegram to his lawyer-manager that read: TRY TO GET HOLD OF A BLOKE CALLED CHAPMAN, CAPLIN OR SOMETHING,

PLAYING SECOND CIRCUIT.

The 'bloke' was none other than Charles Chaplin. And that was the beginning of his career in cinema. Indeed, it took some time for him to touch the sky.

He had the guts to say, 'I have known humiliation. And humiliation is a thing you can never forget.'

In barely three years' time, changing companies one after another—Keystone Films, Essanay Films, and Mutual Films—Chaplin made history. He became an icon.

To start with, Mack Sennett was very strict. Chaplin was asked to be a clown, an object of ridicule and a figure of fun, and just act. But Chaplin remained himself and this made Mack rather uncomfortable. Chaplin soon realised that he needed to conceal his own identity and become a new man. With the help of his make-up and his costume, his persona was changed. This did the trick. On the stage he looked a laughing stock, a butt of jokes. The people watching him laughed uproariously. He was immediately identified as a vagabond, a little man. Mack Sennett was immensely happy. Meanwhile the little man changed his company.

Growing from strength to strength and becoming a celebrity, Chaplin did not have to look back. 'My costume', he said, 'helps me to express my concept of the average man, of almost any man, of myself. The derby is striving for dignity. The moustache is vanity. The tightly buttoned coat and the stick and his whole manner are a gesture towards gallantry and dash and front! He is trying to meet the world bravely to put up a bluff and he knows that too. He knows it so well that he can laugh at himself and pity himself a little.'

And that was how Chaplin's conception of the average man was structured—a fascinating archetype. The persona that grew into being remained

Chaplin and Gandhi

unchanged, his manners the same.

Chaplin's short films, one-reelers or two or more, were made in three years. Most of the matured films that followed shook the world. A number of them, such as *Shoulder Arms* (1918), *The Kid* (1920), *A Woman of Paris* (1923), *The Gold Rush* (1925), *The Circus* (1927), *City Lights* (1931), and *Modern Times* (1936) had a profound influence on viewers. Soon after, when Chaplin was at the height of his glory and was planning a new film, he made an incredible statement: 'In the new film my character will not be quite so nice. I am sharpening the edge of the character so that people who have liked him vaguely will have to make up their minds.'

Did it ever appear that Chaplin would now change over to sound film, which he had not done to date? Image and sound together entwined? Would he then say goodbye to the great mimics like Max Linder, Buster Keaton, and Jacques Tati, with their extraordinary gags and colourful mannerisms—Tati naming their tricks *inspired nonsense*? No, nothing of the kind. He remained the same inimitable Chaplin, with, yes, sound added to the image. How and what for?

The story of Chaplin's entry into 'talking pictures' or 'Talkies' came later when, after *Modern Times*, he thought of *The Great Dictator* (1940). I shall take up that story later, in another chapter.

London, September 1931. Chaplin leaning out of window to see Gandhi

I too knew someone in my own life who embodied the spirit of the eternal vagabond. This goes back many years, to my boyhood. I was born in Faridpur, a small town, now in Bangladesh. In 1938, I passed the Matriculation examination from a local school, and was admitted to college for the two-year Intermediate Science Course. The college had a tennis court for beginners. Believe it or not, I was chosen by the sports teacher, along with five others, to be trained in tennis. I asked my father for a racquet. My father, amused, smiled a bit and, quite sensibly, got me a cheap one. We employed half a dozen ballboys to collect the balls during our practice sessions. So there were these busy boys smartly running around to pick up the balls and throw them to us.

One afternoon, a newcomer, who looked hardly eight or nine, clad in a colourful shirt of rejected cut-pieces collected from a tailor's shop, joined the ballboys. He was not one of our employees. The other ballboys jumped on him—he was an 'outsider'! The boy yelled for help. I rushed up and questioned the attackers. They said that he was not one of them; one complained that he was a Muslim. The boy vehemently protested and pushed the attackers away. He said, 'I have not been circumcised.' Looking straight at me he said, 'You can check if you want.' I stopped him from stripping on the spot, and asked his attackers to let him go.

The name of the boy was Akbar.

He was a pavement dweller, a homeless urchin, often going hungry or surviving on sketchy meals. And he was a vagabond, pure and simple. A roving vagabond.

Soon after, the boy Akbar became a 'friend' of mine. He used to come home with me and was befriended by the whole family—my parents, my brothers and, in particular, my younger sister. Once he stayed with us for a couple of days. My father gave him some money to buy a mat, a pillow, and a sheet. He did so, and slept in our outhouse.

Two days later, Akbar was found missing. His bedding was lying, neatly rolled, in a corner of the outhouse.

A couple of weeks after this, my father saw Akbar near the district court. My father, a leading lawyer, organised, through the owner of a modest eating-house, a meal to be served to the boy whenever he was hungry. However, he seldom asked for food. Akbar kept dropping in at our place, and would accept a bite of something when offered, but he never spent the whole day.

Suddenly, he disappeared from the town. We learnt that he had gone off to a nearby spot where the communists had organised a week-long camp for landless farmers. When he returned, he sang us three or four militant songs, picked up while attending the cultural functions.

Another time, I saw him in a demonstration, vigorously shouting militant slogans like 'Larke Lenge Pakistan' (We'll fight for Pakistan). Our country was still a British colony, and communal tension raised its ugly head more often than not. Yet, when an outbreak of cholera spread through the town and its neighbourhood, and god-fearing Hindus walked the streets and lanes early in the morning chanting hymns to propitiate the gods, Akbar was an inseparable part of the crowd.

And he always kept in touch with me.

There was no end to his stories. When a touring circus came to town, he was paid to distribute leaflets advertising the circus.

And he remained a vagabond all-through.

When I left my home-town and came to Calcutta for further studies, I stayed in a boarding house. Akbar found out my address from my sister. He came and visited me in the boarding house. I was taken aback. Problems notwithstanding, he travelled as a ticketless passenger. He came and saw me in Calcutta a number of times, never paying a paisa for transport. On the contrary, he jumped from one compartment of the train to the other, and earned some money by singing.

Akbar came of age through the years.

A year after the Partition of India, in 1948, my parents left East Bengal, then called East Pakistan, and migrated to a new home in Calcutta.

Akbar also made Calcutta his new home. I wanted him to work as a shoe-shine boy, going from one park to another and earning some money. He worked for a week, but the other boys would not admit this 'outsider'. Not only did he lose the 'job', but the tool kit I had organised for his use was stolen.

On his own, he then managed to get a job as a cook for three or four young clerks, all Muslims, sharing a one-room apartment in Calcutta. I could see Akbar was beginning to grow.

During this time, he would come to our home regularly at noon and read out for my father, then retired, excerpts from his favourite book on the Indian epic The Mahabharata. Nobody, myself included, knew how and when he learnt to read the Bengali script. Perhaps, without his knowing it, he had a streak of extraordinariness in him. Amazing!

My future wife Gita and I knew each other fairly

well by then. She came from a poor family, and I was no better off financially. I told Akbar that I would marry her one day. Akbar was thrilled. He wanted to see her. He managed to get her address from me and met her the very next day. Since winter was approaching, Gita gave him an old blanket. The following day, when he saw me, he was all praise for her 'beautiful eyes'!

Soon after, while crossing a busy street, Akbar was crushed to death between two tramcars. A week later, I came to know about his cruel death from the young men for whom Akbar had been a cook.

When, in 1953, just after my marriage, I wrote my first book on Chaplin, I dedicated it to the memory of my eternal vagabond, Akbar.

3

Looking back, 'to tell the tale' left untold ...

Looking back, *Making a Living* [1914] was Chaplin's first film. His second appearance was in *Kid Auto Races at Venice* [1914]. The first film, around 1000 feet in length, had a comparatively well-developed storyline, but his costume, make-up and character had nothing in common with the figure of Charlie as we know it. In the opinion of a British trade journal, *Kid Auto Races* was the funniest film they had ever seen. Having watched several of his films of approximately the same length the journal observed that Chaplin was a born comedian who had done things they had never seen on the screen before.

One after another, in quick succession, he acted in eight more films, ten in all, none of them directed by him. As for other comedians on screen, Max Linder [1883–1925] and Buster Keaton [1895–1966] came earlier and Jacques Tati [1907–1982] years later. All of them were comic entertainers, clowns indulging in jests and antics and playfulness, with their own mannerisms, writing their own gags and jokes, even ad-libbing as required—like Charles Chaplin. But, to a greater degree than usual, Chaplin was a perfectionist; his mannerisms, body language, and expressions were inimitably *Chaplinesque*. According to Jacques Tati, Chaplin's was a *creative game* that could be deemed *inspired nonsense*. Such a phrase as this was not far from, for example, Lewis Carroll's *nonsense verse* in literature, a form of non-moralising rhythmical text aimed basically at children. Every bit was laughable, comical, infused with buffoonery. The spectators were infinitely happy.

Film after film Chaplin started growing from strength to strength. When, later, he started directing his own films with no break, he made it a point to see that every detail was worked out faultlessly. So much so that every shot had to have plenty of 'takes' and 're-takes', every sequence was redone and restructured many times, and a complete set was even pulled down and re-built over and over again. Not to speak of unfit actors who would be summarily dismissed at his command. That was when Chaplin didn't have to worry about exposing 100,000 feet of celluloid or more to make a film 2000 feet long. It was an incredibly high ratio, seldom shot by any of his contemporaries. Even in its final shape he would reject a large chunk if he found it redundant or unpleasing. Finally, after a film met his fullest satisfaction, he would issue strict orders that shots, sequences, sets—whatever he had scrapped as useless—were to be totally destroyed.

Now, to understand the times, Chaplin blended fact, fiction, and fantasy in order to create an effect of frolic and pleasure. But to relate this to contemporaneity was what he always looked for, and this led him to construct a fully developed story, with content and form walking hand in hand.

That was a time when, with every onward movement, as if climbing a steep hill, the horizon kept changing. That was when his views and character were given ever-increasing dimensions. When, comicality apart, he appeared unhappy, indigent, baffled and frustrated under it all. In terms of construction, everything looked fresh and healthy.

At the end of each film, more often than not,

with a carefree philosophical shrug of his shoulders, Charlie walked away towards the glowing horizon—'a fallen aristocrat at grips with poverty expressing his conception of the average man, of almost any man, of myself.' Admittedly, it was a novel way of understanding the times and history.

The wheels of history kept turning. Film after film was made. Various sorts of experiences occurred in the life of 'the average man'. And, as he always did, he kept on lampooning himself.

Either lampooning, or feeling lonely and sad. Or, for that matter, also confronting cannibal time. Somewhere along the way, belying hopes and beliefs, he turned out to be a part of history himself. Life turned from bad to worse, clouds remained cloudy, the sun did not break through and darkness deepened.

War came [World War One: 1914–1918]. Along came *Shoulder Arms* [1918], a new comedy, with Charlie, now a soldier-in-the-making, lashing out at the soul-killing business of war in a manner that was typically Chaplinesque. To fight for democracy he laid down his favourite cane, bravely picked up the rifle, and trained himself as a soldier with the Allies. At a certain point of time, fighting all alone, he saw that he was besieged by a number of Germans. When asked how he had captured 13 of them single-handed, pat came the reply, 'I surrounded them.' Applying trick after trick, always Chaplinesque, and following success after success in the battle encounters, he climbed down into the dugouts, and keeping himself hidden inside the trenches, battled against the Germans. Finally, outwitting everybody around, Charlie brought the Kaiser to the Allied camp. Instantly a title filled the screen: AND PEACE TO THE WORLD.

In this way a *creative game*, punctuated with a host of *inspired nonsense*, came to an end with slapstick at its scintillating height, with everything in perfect rhythm.

The film was released three weeks before the Versailles Treaty [1919] was signed between the Allies and Germany. It was a big success, one of the greatest successes in Chaplin's career. And, as everybody knows, nothing succeeds like success.

Having made a couple of more films after *Shoulder Arms*, which were rather sceptically received, *The Kid*

[1921] was his next big hit. It was the story of Charlie and a kid, 'a picture with a smile, and perhaps a tear.' It was a story built in simple continuity without much revision of the original version. And unlike his earlier productions, it was an hour-long film.

A Jitney Elopement

Coincidentally, the first film I ever saw was *The Kid*. I was seven at the time. In an annual fair in my hometown, now in Banglasesh, I saw the film along with two of my elder brothers and our parents. Our parents laughed heartily, as did my brothers and I. I laughed and laughed and laughed. And then, neatly and cleanly, I forgot all about the film. I did not remember the film for long because initially, even in my adolescence and for few years after, I had practically no interest in films except for reading books on various subjects with no particular specialisation, no direction. I must confess that I became a filmmaker by accident when, unknowingly, I bumped once into a book on the aesthetics of cinema. It was not that I understood the book in its entirety, but it led me to continue reading many more books on cinema and society, all in the then Imperial Library—later, after Independence, called the National Library. That was when I developed a passion for reading films, watching films, writing on films, not to speak of Charles Chaplin alone, and, eventually, making films. And that, for sure, is a different story.

To come back to Chaplin and *The Kid*—with a male child in her arms, a young woman, sad and forlorn, was seen coming out of a charity hospital. Looking around she found a beautiful car parked outside. She left the child in the back of the car with a note for the finder, if any, to protect and care for him. Two crooks who were in a hurry to steal the car found the baby. They picked him up and dumped him in a nearby garbage can and drove away with the car. Charlie appeared on the scene and heard the baby crying in the garbage can. He picked up the baby and gently put him in another car. The owner of the car was annoyed and asked the tramp to take away the pest. Now, with the baby back in his arms, Charlie was touched by the short note. He had no choice but to look around to see what else could he do other than rearing him up in the best possible manner. With affection that the child deserved, in spite of himself, Charlie turned foster-father.

After five years, the tramp remained unchanged, with his new gift, a 'son'. Jackie, then a five-year-old, was his most talented disciple. To earn their livelihood amidst untold miseries, the two joined forces and continued performing their *creative games* one after another with the cops chasing them and being baffled most of the time. The battle had its ups and downs, and the dramatics were very cleverly designed. But, ultimately, Charlie and Jackie lost the battle and were ruthlessly separated. Did they meet ever again? Yes, they met in a celestial dream! And they met once again.

The Kid was completed and released. Jackie Coogan [1914–1984] became famous as a child actor. Now, with no plan chalked out, Chaplin decided for the first time to come back to Britain. Did he feel tired of working so hard over the years? He was reported to have said, 'I need an emotional stimulus.'

His new job

The Kid

Incidentally, there is a popular story about the discovery of Jackie Coogan which, I feel, deserves retelling. It goes thus: Once, strolling down the road, Chaplin noticed a boy, sitting on the corner, peeling bananas, and throwing the peels one after another into the middle of the road, clearly in the hope that one or two passersby would slip and fall, much to the boy's delight.

Chaplin watched all this, standing behind the boy. He asked him if he could meet his father. Looking up, the boy asked, 'Why?' Chaplin said, 'I want you to act in my next film.' The boy replied confidently that he himself could take the decision, because he was already five years old.

Quite possibly, this is as much of an apocryphal anecdote as the one which, during my days in Scottish Church College, I read in an 'authentic and authorised' biography of Swami Vivekananda, written by a radical journalist of repute, Satyendranath Majumdar, the editor of a leading Bengali daily with large circulation. While reading, I bumped eventually into an anecdote of Swamiji when he was still a boy in school. His nickname was Biley. Biley was pretty friendly with the family coachman, who was from Bihar. The coachman once confided in him the sad story of his own married life; he said that his wife was cruel to him. Biley was deeply moved. He rushed out, grabbed hold of the idol of Rama and his consort Sita to whom his mother was devoted and worshipped regularly. Holding the idol roughly in one hand, Biley went up to the terrace. The mother was there, hanging out clothes to dry. Without paying her any heed, Biley, in order to crush the idol, threw it down from the roof. The author commented that, instead of rebuking the boy, Biley's mother kept quiet, wondering at her son; it seems that she could see the vision of a 'saint' in his face, a saint-in-the making!

Reading this piece I felt rather uncomfortable. The next day, on impulse, I went to their ancestral house where Swamiji's two brothers, both very old, were still alive. Mahendra Dutta, the elder, was religious, wrote remarkable books on Swamiji; but the youngest was made of different stuff.

I met him, the youngest of the three brothers, Dr Bhupendranath Dutta, younger than Swami Vivekananda by eighteen years, who, due to age, was critically ill. Dr Bhupen Dutta was a renowned thinker and writer, the author of several books on the social sciences, including *Studies in Indian Social Polity* which I had read immediately on its publication and highly admired. I found it fascinating for its originality. When, earlier, I went to see him, I plucked up enough courage to narrate the story of the coachman and Swamiji (or, as he was then, Biley) and of the Rama-Sita idol being crushed. Very respectfully did I ask him if their mother could possibly have reacted in the way the author had suggested. I did not conceal the fact that I thought not.

Dr Dutta listened to me smilingly and asked me to come closer. He patted me on the shoulder and said quietly, 'Keep it up, comrade! And never forget that, being an extraordinary man, there are many such apocryphal stories about Swamiji.' As indeed there are about Chaplin!

Chaplin rushed to New York to board the ship bound for London. Both in New York and during his journey by ship, Chaplin, then a world figure, faced plenty of questions, most of which he evaded, smartly answering only a few. When asked if he was a Bolshevik, he said: 'I am an artist. I am interested in life. Bolshevism is a new phase of life. I must be interested in it.'

London, 1921. The gruesome slum in the south of London where a family of four was reduced to two—mother and son. Through a window they would observe their world, the world that projected itself with passion and despair in the films of Chaplin.

So, after a lapse of seven frenzied years, once again London, in 1921. It was as if a door in Chaplin had been flung open and there were no limits to his exploration—of his childhood, of his adolescence. So many things flashed past in a series of memories. Referring to children he came across he recalled his own past and said: 'As I pass, they look up. Frankly and without embarrassment they look at me with their beautiful kindly eyes. They smile at me, I smile back. Oh, if only I could do something for them! These waifs with scarcely any chance at all.'

Remembering the old singer, blind and a pauper, Chaplin 'learnt the rare beauty of his song (*You are my honey, honeysuckle*) which had gladdened and haunted me (in my childhood).' He recognised the same man walking along the street, older by seven years, and in a bad way. Chaplin mentioned him in his *My Trip Abroad* [1922]. He said: 'To me it is too horrible. He is the personification of poverty at its worst, sunk in that inertia that comes of lost hope ...' And there he stood outside a park and memories were magically conjured up and surfaced, image following image, event following event. He remembered how, in the summer of 1908, he fell in love for the first time. He was nineteen and the girl was fifteen. An adolescent infatuation? A first heartbreak?

In a solemn manner out came Chaplin's words: 'Kennington Gate! That has its memories. Sad, sweet, rapidly recurring memories.'

The girl, then fifteen, was born in Bristol. Her mother, planning a stage career for her and two more children, brought all three to London. The mother got in touch with the head of Karno's company and had no problem getting the fifteen-year-old daughter admitted. One day the girl was rehearsing with Karno's troupe, when Chaplin, himself part of the same team, standing in the wings, saw her—'a slim gazelle, with shapely oval face, a bewitching smile and beautiful teeth.'

David Robinson [b. 1930], esteemed author and journalist, described the affair in some detail in his scrupulously researched volume, *Chaplin–His Life and Art* [1985]. Robinson said: 'For anyone else it would have been an adolescent infatuation, a temporary heartbreak forgotten in a week. But Chaplin was not like anyone else, and something in his sensibilities rooted in the deprivations of his childhood caused this encounter to leave a deep impression upon him. The object of his feeling was a girl called Henrietta (Hetty) Florence Kelly.'

Robinson says, of the brief affair, that Hetty, while rehearsing, did not see Chaplin watching her from the wings. When she came off the stage, she saw him standing there behind the wings. She asked him to hold a mirror for her. The following night, Wednesday, he asked her if she would agree to meet on Sunday afternoon. She agreed. Next day, Thursday, Chaplin, before he escorted Hetty back home, drew three pounds from his bank. But the evening was a minor fiasco since Hetty had eaten and Chaplin had no appetite. Walking with her to Camberwell he experienced a new kind of joy—'I was walking in Paradise with inner blissful excitement.'

Chaplin continued collecting and escorting her on Friday and Saturday, and when, at last, he met her in the park on Sunday, Hetty was distant and nervous and would not hold his hand. She told him that she was too young and that he was asking too much of her. Talk of love puzzled and alarmed her.

Chaplin could not resist walking to Camberwell Road the next morning, but instead of Hetty he met her mother, who said that Hetty had come home crying. He asked to see her, and the mother at first refused. When she relented, and he went with her to the house, he found Hetty cold and unfriendly.

Chaplin did not understand what had happened. The answer may be that her mother did not intend her beautiful daughter to be wasted on a little vaudeville comedian with no prospects. Within a very few years, she was to see her three daughters married to men with money and position. From first sight to farewell, the affair had lasted eleven days, and they had never been together for more than twenty minutes. Chaplin never forgot; and both in his life and art he seemed for many years to be trying to recapture the ecstasy he had felt in the company of Hetty Kelly ... .

Thus the eleven-day-affair came to an end. The contact was lost for years, the worlds between them too vast to breach.

Strangely, ten years later, in July 1918, when Chaplin was busy with *Shoulder Arms*, he received a letter from Hetty, then somewhere in America with her husband. The letter began with the line, 'Do you remember a silly young girl ... ?'

Hetty's letter was misplaced and remained untraced, but, strangely, not the torn envelope with her address. Besides, the first line of the untraced letter was unforgettable.

If not the letter, Chaplin's reply, just a few days after the receipt, survived. He wrote, 'Dear Hetty, it is always the unexpected that happens, both in moving pictures and in real life. You can never imagine what an unexpected pleasure it was for me when I discovered your letter on my desk this morning. At first, when I caught sight of the envelope, my pulse quickened ... I quickly tore open the envelope and—Lo and Behold!—it was from you. You, above all people, to hear from and after so many years! I was certainly thrilled, and yet I half expected you to write sometime or other because of the interesting events that have taken place in our lives; and, after all, to hear from one's old friends is a great pleasure ...

'Well, Hetty, you have not changed a particle. By that I mean your personality—it is manifest on every page of your letter ... you ask me how I am, etc., etc.. Well, physically I am perfect; morally—well, I am all that could be desired for a young man of twenty-nine years. I am still a bachelor, that is not my fault ...

'Do you remember, Hetty, I once told you that money and success were not everything. At the time I had not had the experience of either, but I felt it was so, and now I have experienced both. I find that the pursuit of happiness can only be had from within ourselves and the interest of others ...

'But enough of this philosophy. How about

yourself? I sincerely hope you have fully recovered by now, and are in pink of condition. You must take greater care of yourself ... I shall be anxiously counting the days until I hear from you, so please write and let me know that you are well and smiling again. Yours ever, Charlie.'

A week passed, then a month, then a year, with no reply. And surprisingly and unaccountably, nor was there one ever after.

Back to London in 1921. There Chaplin heard that Hetty Kelly had died on 4 November 1918, a week before the Armistice. Chaplin knew nothing about the terrible news until he came to London.

Once again Chaplin disembarked from a taxi in front of the park where he had had his appointment with Hetty. He wrote in his diary: '(I remember) how I was dolled up in my tight-fitting frock coat, hat and cane. I was quite the dude as I watched every street car until four o'clock, waiting for Hetty to step off, smiling as she saw me waiting. I stood for a few moments at the gate. My taxi driver thought I was mad. But I was forgetting the taxi drivers. I was seeing a lad of nineteen, dressed to the pink, with fluttering heart, waiting for the moment of the day when he and happiness walked along the road. The road is alluring now. It beckons for another walk, and as I hear a street car approaching, I turn eagerly for a moment almost expecting to see the same trim Hetty step off, smiling. The car stops. A couple of men get out. An old woman. Some children. But no Hetty. Hetty is gone. So is the lad with the frock coat and cane.'

Later, Chaplin wrote further, 'How depressing to me are all parks! The loneliness of them! One never goes to a park unless one is lonesome. And lonesomeness is sad. The symbol of sadness, that is a park.'

Thus the tender little story of Hetty, 'the silly young girl', and 'the lad with the frock coat' came to an end: 'Sad, sweet, rapidly recurring memories'.

Paulette Goddard in *Modern Times*

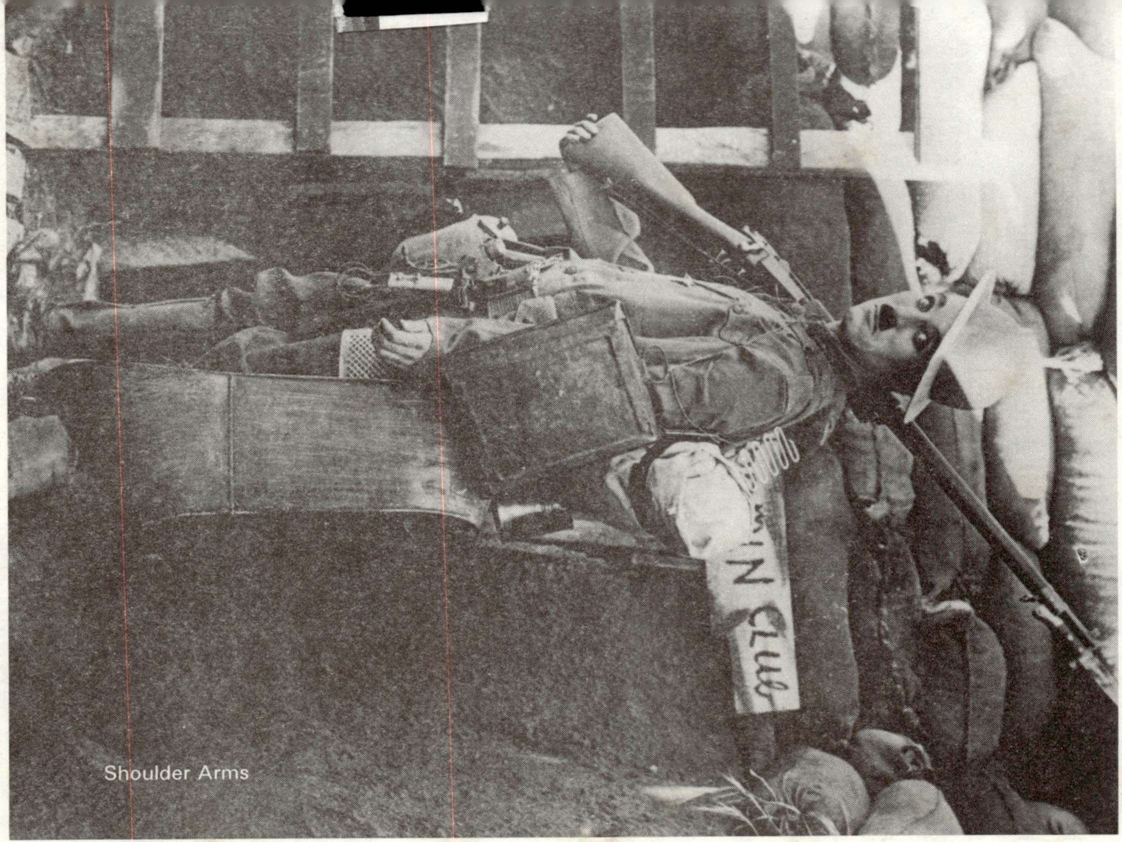

Shoulder Arms

4

Still on the move he disappears over the horizon to the promised land ...

If one thinks of the films Chaplin made from the beginning of his career, including the three he made after *The Kid*, one that was very different in many ways was *A Woman of Paris* [1923]. It was different because Chaplin did not appear in that film except for a few seconds as an unnamed porter. It was unusual because there was no *Chaplinesque* chase in its rhythm and hardly any *inspired nonsense*; because there was no shrugging of shoulders or journey off to a promised land against the glowing sunset, although the viewers could not resist peals of laughter when the film provoked them to respond to lighter moments. Which was why, unlike in his earlier films, Chaplin cautiously started this particular film with a short introduction which said: 'Humanity is composed not of heroes and villains but of men and women and all their passions, good and bad, given them by God.

They sin only in blindness and the ignorant condemn their mistakes, but the wise pity them.'

A Woman of Paris was Chaplin's first serious drama, a very different film in every possible manner—both in content and form. With no clowning, no trickery, no buffoonery whatsoever. A different film and a really challenging one.

In a special programme note, he said: 'I have striven for realism, true to life. As I personally see it, life has its beauty, sadness ... gaiety. All these are necessary to make life interesting ... .' About the story, he made it unpretentiously clear that it was to be 'intimate, simple and human, presenting a problem as old as the ages—showing it with as much of truth as I am allowed to put into it, giving it a treatment as near realism as I have been able to devise for a better understanding of human frailties.' Further, he told an eminent New York journalist: 'As much as I have noticed life in its dramatic climaxes, men and women try to hide their emotions rather than seek to express them.'

All this was evident in *A Woman of Paris*, as projected in the situations and the characters. Chaplin, in his treatment of the subject-matter, built the image of life in its truest shape with utmost restraint. But he had his doubts about it being considered too moralistic. That was exactly what he kept an eye out for.

After the serious introduction, the film started with a woman in a tranquil village in France—simple, sweet and serene. She was deeply in love with a young man aspiring to be an artist. They had absolutely no problem between them but both the parents of the budding artist and the young woman stood fiercely in their way, unbearably arrogant conformists and terribly obstinate.

The couple resolved to leave the village and run away to Paris, but to little avail. Hoping against hope, she waited for the young man at the railway station. The train to Paris stopped at the station and left. The woman, sad and forlorn, was still standing on the platform, the lights from the coaches rapidly reflecting light and darkness on her face. Which, regardless of the absence of the passing sound of the train, gave the impression that they would never meet. Later on, she went alone to Paris, and he had no choice but to live with his parents.

A year passed ...

Appeared a subtitle: 'Paris—the magic city, where fortune is fickle and a woman gambles with life.'

What was inevitable had happened. Forced to change her persona, she became a woman of Paris, living a fast life, but with a dual personality.

At last, collecting enough courage, the budding artist left the village and met his fiancée. He did not feel that she had changed. He was happy and he drew a portrait of her. And, 'lo and behold, it was a portrait of the woman that she had been—simple, sweet and serene ... .'

The ending, however, was an unfortunate tragedy.

Edna Purviance [1895–1985], one of Chaplin's most favourite actresses, played the female lead, giving an excellent performance. The viewers liked the film, though not all loved it. Was it because *A Woman of Paris* was too moralistic, as Chaplin was afraid of? Emotions too loud? Not adequately controlled?

Once again, Chaplin came back to his own world—with his 'concept of the average man, of any man'—as the impeccable Charlie, immaculately made up and costumed with the bowler hat on his head, his inimitable footwear, his toothbrush-like moustache, the tightly buttoned coat, a stick in hand and his whole manner befittingly *Chaplinesque*.

Chaplin hoped that *The Gold Rush* [1925] would be 'the picture I would like to be remembered by'. A vast expanse of desolate ice and snow with Charlie, a lone prospector, walking through it all in search of gold. Never succumbing to exhaustion, the unwavering Charlie braved the ice field to reach his goal.

The Gold Rush

In a different context and in a manner far removed from the world of *The Gold Rush*, I made a film based on a class-divided society in 1965, about an unemployed young man 'at grips with poverty'. In a desperate bid to cross the wealth barrier the young man indulged in a serio-comic game which finally came to a sticky end. I called it *Akash Kusum* (Up in the Clouds). Contrarily, or, in other words, intensifying the denial of what I would say about *The Gold Rush* or my *Akash Kusum*, the great poet and prophet Rabindranath Tagore wrote a highly perceptive poem which started with:

Tora je ja bolish bhai
amar sonar harin chai.

Say whatever you have to, dear,
say it without fear,
and no wonder, I need a golden deer.

The reference to the golden deer is from the Indian epic, *The Ramayana*. 'Mareech' is the name of the deer, astonishingly illusive.

While washing his own pyjamas in his grim wash basin the protagonist of my film *Akash Kusum* was heard humming this song to himself. Thereafter

he came to downtown to meet his friend, an executive with a business firm. He and his friend took a lift up to the topmost floor of a sky-kissing high-rise. They walked onto the terrace and looked out. Viewing the vast cityscape stretching up to the horizon the protagonist of the film threw up his arms in ecstasy and exclaimed, his words tumbling out, 'Damn it, I'll buy the whole city all by myself!!!' He was, and still is, a fascinating actor—Soumitra Chatterjee.

Appeared a subtitle in *The Gold Rush*: 'Man proposes but storm disposes.'

Suddenly, a strong wind was heralded by a terrifying flash of lightning. A raging storm unsettled all that was calm and quiet until it blurred the horizon; and Charlie, the lone prospector, disappeared from the scene. There was no trace of him. He was simply eclipsed.

The violent storm threw him into a hideout where he found a devil-may-care sort of fellow. The man threw him out but the storm outside pushed him back to confront the man again. This pushing in and throwing out continued for some time, with the storm still raging outside, until another man was blown into the hideout along with his ramshackle tent. The tent within the hideout—a room within a room. The three continued fighting among themselves, with the storm still raging unabated. Finally, fatigued, they made a truce.

Anger subsided but hunger began to ferment. The man with the ramshackle tent, a criminal, rushed out in search of food and never came back. The devil-may-care sort of fellow and Charlie looked helplessly at each other in impotent despair. Unless they could organise food, they would die of hunger for sure.

Having no option, Charlie pulled off one of his favourite boots and, in utter desperation, boiled it. He started tearing the boiled boot to pieces—nails, leather and the softest part, the insole, and laces too. He tore it all into separate pieces and strips and arranged them on the plate. He consumed it all with relish. Even the nails were licked clean.

The devil-may-care sort of fellow watched Charlie as he was busy chewing, swallowing and eating and even licking the nails. Unbearably provoked to hallucination by the sight of the happy man, he flew into a rage and jumped on Charlie as though he was a plump hen to be eaten. This monstrous game continued for a little while. The hungry man chased and the other intermittently played hen—a remarkably choreographed work of hallucination in perfect Chaplinesque rhythm!

Despite the non-stop fury of the elements and more gags in the vast expanse of ice, there was no sign of gold anywhere. Undaunted, Charlie left the ice field and came to a town with no money and no hope either, with one foot tightly bandaged because he had eaten up the boot.

A chance meeting with a charming dancing girl in a hotel changed his life. But it did not last long. Nevertheless, Charlie invited the dancing girl to a cosy meal in a cosy corner to celebrate the New Year's Eve. The girl agreed to come. He was overjoyed.

Everything was ready—table, place settings, plates. But she was yet to come. Of course she would. Charlie remained seated at the head of the table, and waited. Waiting and dreaming, he took two forks from the table in two hands. With care and caution, and with intense love, he speared two bread rolls with his forks and continued to gently move his hands in a delightful movement which, in the history of Chaplin's aesthetics, came to be known as the 'Dance of the Rolls'. Terrific! A brilliant feat in Chaplin's oeuvre!

At long last, Charlie and the sweet dancing girl met. They embraced each other. She smiled and he smiled back.

The Gold Rush was a phenomenal success all over the world, received everywhere with tremendous enthusiasm. The French intellectuals in particular—

April 1924. *The Gold Rush*. Location filming at Truckee in the Sierra Nevada, California. Chaplin with his assistant, Eddie Sutherland

Louis Aragon, Rene Clair, Germaine Dulac, Man Ray and others—went mad over the film.

In the same year, 1925, a young man in his twenties, the stout and short Sergei Eisenstein [1898–1948], revolutionised the world of cinema by making *Battleship Potemkin* in the erstwhile Soviet Union. He and his contemporaries—Pudovkin, Dovzenko

and others including the eminent poet Mayakovsky [1893–1930]—were all wild about Chaplin. In his heart to heart talk with himself (in Jay Leyda's *Kino*), Mayakovsky asked—How did foreign films beat

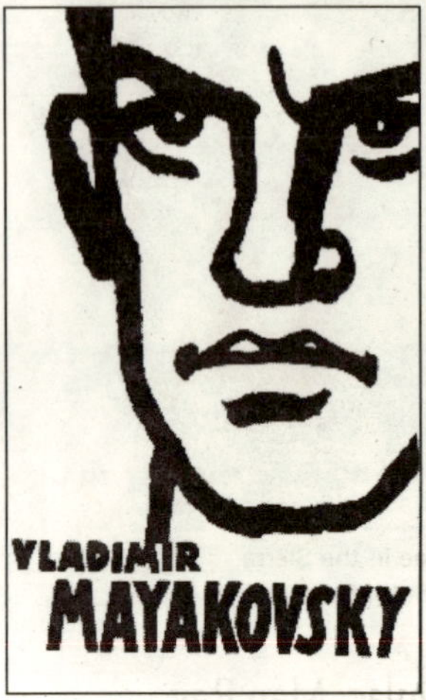

theirs, both generally and in artistic quality? He said to himself: 'Foreign films use special means that derive from film technique, which cannot be found in any other medium of expression. And Chaplin was a man of great artistic vision, and that was why the transformation of Chaplin into a chicken in *The Gold Rush* was possible, and in another film, *A Woman of Paris*, the woman standing on the railway platform and the passing train continuously throwing light on her face lending the impression that she would not meet her fiancé ever again could be so beautifully constructed.' Besides this, Eisenstein's long essay on *The Kid* turned out to be highly readable stuff, both for academics and learners.

And what about Charlie? Travelling a long way, he was still alive and kicking. But the problems in

The Circus

Chaplin's private life deepened for one reason or the other. Though this did not deter him from making his next film, *The Circus* [1928], the seven-reeler took a fairly long time because of family problems which cast a strain even over the production work. As a result, the quality of the film suffered substantially.

Anyway, coming to *The Circus*, Charlie managed to get a job in a travelling circus, did his duty, did all that he was asked to, did every bit of hackwork, even tight-rope walking—which flopped—everything that was needed to please the owner and the sweet girl on the trapeze. Finally, in an unguarded moment, he had a fall and landed in a corner of the cage housing the circus lion. In the other corner of the cage the lion was resting undisturbed. For Charlie there was no way to escape.

Outside, the dog barked, the girl on the trapeze screamed, others held their breath, some were running helter-skelter, but none of them could be of any help in rescuing poor Charlie.

The lion looked at the crowd outside, stood up, yawned and ambled across to the other corner to smell Charlie.

Outside, the crowd was scared to death, but no one spoke a word, or made a sound. Silence prevailed all around. A dreadful silence!

The lion sniffed to examine if the man smelled good enough to eat. In utter repugnance, he turned back and walked away to the other corner. Appeared a short subtitle: 'Unfit for consumption'!!!

Finally, the tent was dismantled. The circus came to an end. The people and the animals were pushed into the trucks to be dumped outside the station for the next performance. The girl on the trapeze asked Charlie to come with them. But he did not. The trucks left, leaving Charlie behind.

He was ready to go his own way ... to meet his destiny.

1928—the year that made history in the world of cinema. Following continuous experiments for years in the audio-visual medium, sound, at last, found a permanent place in cinema. On 8 July 1928, Warner Brothers of Hollywood had shown in New York the first 'talking picture', and called it *Lights of New York*. Audiences all over the world went mad with the advent of the phenomenal 'talkie'. But Chaplin was still conscious of the technical shortcomings of the new development, and, in the early stages, of the unimaginative and inartistic use of the new medium. So much so that even at the beginning of 1931 he was still declaring that he would give the talkies three more years. He knew how much he had to lose if he was forced into talking pictures. He believed, and he had absolutely no doubt about it, that he had made the silent pantomime into an international language.

He had proved that the gestures, the expressions, the twists and twitches, the thoughts, the feelings of the Little Tramp were readily comprehensible to all, even to the vast audiences of America and Europe and elsewhere in the world. He had a fear that speech would instantly rob the figure of its universality.

So, till then, Chaplin was undecided about sound. Soon after, he slightly modified his opinion, and said: 'Dialogue may or may not have a place in comedy. What I merely said was, the dialogue does not have a place in the sort of comedies I make. For myself, I know that I cannot use dialogue.'

Further, when an interviewer asked Chaplin if he would ever try it, he said, 'I have never tried jumping off the monument in Trafalgar Square, but I have a definite idea that it would be 'unhealthful'.' He continued, saying, 'For years I have specialised in one type of comedy, strictly pantomime. I have measured it, gauged it, studied it. I have been able to establish exact principles to govern its effect on audiences. It has a certain pace and tempo. Dialogue, to my way of thinking, always slows action, because action must wait upon words.'

However, though he was firm in his public statements, Chaplin, in the privacy of his studio, was clearly less convinced. In a few years, for external reasons and political pressure, he was to change his opinion. But Chaplin did not use sound in his next film, *City Lights* [1931], except for a few cinematic effects and the introduction of a background score which was entirely his own composition.

City Lights—'A Comedy Romance in Pantomime'—was based in a metropolitan city which could be located anywhere in the West.

It was early in the morning. The central park of the city was beautifully decorated and the chosen elite of some social standing came to witness the unveiling of the statue of a great woman, with two footmen standing on either side. A subtitle filled the screen—TO THE PEOPLE OF THE CITY WE DONATE THIS MONUMENT: PEACE AND PROSPERITY.

As, with fanfare, the statue was unveiled, someone was seen sleeping on her lap. Sleeping as if he was dreaming. The dignitaries were aghast. Raging with fury, they threw him out. It was none other than Charlie, the eternal Tramp.

Charlie continued walking away, as always.

I saw not one single statue or monument in my small town, now in Bangladesh. When, in the early forties, I came to Calcutta to study Physics, I saw plenty of them, scattered in important parks, at the four-point crossing of Park Street-Chowringhee Road-Mayo Road-Outram Road, also at the intersection of Dalhousie and Council House Street and other junctions, all in the central part of the city. They lent a special distinction to the metropolis during the British rule in India.

A couple of years later, I saw Chaplin's *City Lights* in a city theatre. I hugely enjoyed the brilliant sequence of the unveiling of the statue of 'Peace and Prosperity' with Charlie sleeping on the lap of the woman and possibly dreaming.

A comparison to Michelangelo's (and Salvador Dali's) classic 'Pieta' occurred to me—Holy Divine Mother Mary looking down with serene eyes at her eternally sleeping god-child, Christ, on her lap.

I was wondering why so far no Indian filmmaker had poked fun at any of the statues in Calcutta, which was branded by Lord Clive, the founder of the British Empire in India, as 'The most wicked place in the world.'

The time came few years after the foreign rulers abandoned the city and left the country in 1947.

In 1968, in one of the decolonising drives by the Left-wing ruling parties in West Bengal, the Left Government removed the Imperial Dignitaries from the important junctions of the streets and parks. All these dignitaries, with a couple of equestrian statues amongst them, were uprooted, chained, and loaded onto big open trucks. And then some of them were planted unceremoniously, as if under house arrest, in the sprawling gardens surrounding the huge memorial to the onetime Empress of India, Queen Victoria [1819 – 1901]. The most of the others were left unattended at Barrackpore in the deserted garden-house of one of the Viceroys of British India. It was both great fun, and, for obvious reasons, harsh and bitter. The entire operation was captured on 35mm celluloid by a friend of mine but he did not use it. When, later, I was very much in circulation, I directed three consecutive films, *Calcutta Trilogy* [1970 – 1973], and there I made extensive use of the footage. To my mind, that was an effective way of understanding my time and history—past and present—both funny and bitter.

After the introductory sequence, i.e., the unveiling of the statue, a kind of a starter, so to say, *City Lights* played principally with three characters—the iconic Charlie, a blind pavement florist with whom he built a tentative relationship, and a millionaire with a dual personality—tough and hard-hearted during the daytime and a philanthropic hilarious drunkard at night. By night Charlie was his regular friend and philosopher and a dependable night-guard. During the day, when he was sober, the millionaire could not recognise his nocturnal chum.

City Lights—location filming

Charlie used to see the blind pavement florist selling flowers to passersby. When Charlie had some money, he bought a flower or two, not more. One day a car passed by at high speed. Charlie saw the millionaire seated in the limousine, looking out, but he never even noticed the 'vagabond'. Charlie looked at him and nonchalantly crossed the road to buy a flower. That was all, and she was happy. Charlie escorted her to her grandmother's modest shack.

At night the millionaire, dead-drunk, decided to commit suicide, but his friend and philosopher embraced him and said: 'Tomorrow the birds will sing! Be brave! Face life!' As advised, he continued to play the sober millionaire by day, and by night he was wild as ever.

Slapsticks and gags went on for a period, in the true Chaplinesque manner, provoking fun and laughter, until one day Charlie's attention was drawn to an advertisement about an ophthalmologist who, by dint of courage and conviction, could successfully return eyesight to the blind. But the medical fee was prohibitive. Despite insurmountable difficulties, he approached his millionaire friend and benefactor and got a large amount of money which he immediately passed on to the pavement girl. As luck would have it, he was chased by the police for stealing money and thrown into jail. When he was released, he straightway came to the pavement, but the florist was not to be found. He picked out a flower from the pavement, remembering the past. His attention was drawn to a fancy shop and he was pleasantly surprised to see the florist, now the owner of the big shop, watching him. Ah, it was she, with her sight fully restored!

Charlie came to the door with the garbage-flower in his hand and looked at the owner of the flower shop. He did not have the courage to tell her who he was, and she, mistaking him for a beggar, forced in his hand some money and a flower with sympathy and compassion. The moment she touched his fingers, she got a shock. All choked up, she whispered, 'Who are you?' Quietly Chaplin the vagabond and the tramp said, 'So, you can see!' And the girl replied with a double-entendre, 'Yes, I can see now.'

Bernard Shaw, as I said before, saw the film premiered in 1931 in London in Chaplin's company. It was a huge success. Shaw laughed and cried—he loved the film. In the American premiere too, Einstein did the same—crying and laughing.

While in London, Shaw tried to convince Chaplin when they were talking one-to-one that though true art is not propaganda, propaganda is an essential adjunct in matters of art. Chaplin did not agree. Strongly opinionated as he was, he asserted that art should and must be art—and always the same. However, he changed his opinion soon after, when he confronted the violent reality of the years ahead, when hope and faith seemed terribly suspect, and when the global crisis deepened beyond comprehension.

In spite of the happy ending of *City Lights*, Chaplin remained the same, the inimitable Charlie walking on his unbeaten way. He was now found in a new environment in his new film, *Modern Times* [1936]. The film started with a flock of sheep being herded, as if on their way to the slaughterhouse—followed by the next visual of workers streaming out of a factory.

Charlie was found loafing around in the factory area. Without quite knowing how, he got inducted as a worker. He worked hard, without even a moment to have his lunch, or even to urinate. Every other person in the factory was in the same condition, working hard and earning a pittance. But, unlike the other workers, Charlie made a mess of everything. The gags were there, but these were all machine-made gags, never seen before. When the workers stood outside the factory and got involved in a massive strike with a charter of trade union demands, Charlie was with the angry workers. Police rushed in and violently dispersed the strikers. Charlie was still there, looking around. In the pandemonium, a lorry made its way through the crowd. A cautionary tell-tale (red) flag fell from the lorry, unnoticed by the driver. Charlie picked up the flag and followed the running vehicle. The police caught him by the neck because they thought he was the leader of the strikers. Every bit of the event was built up with utmost care and efficiency. So, without his knowing what it was all about, Charlie was thrown into jail. A brilliant sequence. And the spectators just laughed and laughed.

Time passed. Charlie was released from jail. Life in prison was pleasant because he did not have to worry about food. He was heartbroken to be free. He did his best to get arrested again, but the police was of no help. Disappointed, he went his own way. He met a girl who has just escaped from an orphanage. They became friends. He earned a bit and they started living in a rickety hut with a lake not too far away. Just to please himself, and the girl, Charlie stood by the lake and launched into a perfect dive. Unfortunately, the water was knee-deep. The girl laughed and Charlie smiled. Once again, an instance of *inspired nonsense*!

Followed many gags and friskiness. Finally, Charlie and the girl had nothing to do but walk on. Hand in hand, Charlie assured the girl, 'We will get along.' And continued to walk with confident steps.

Modern Times, when it was released, was received extremely well. The people made note of the revolutionary change in Chaplin's attitude to individuals and society. But there were others who saw leftist tendencies in the film. They found *Modern Times* intolerable. On the other hand, diehard communists in the Soviet Union were critical of the film because, they conjectured, Chaplin could not accept technological advances made in society.

Chaplin was instantly annoyed. He said: 'This

makes no sense at all. I was only poking fun at the general confusion from which we are all suffering .... The things I tried to say in this film are very close to everyone. I know of a factory where the workers were fined if they went to the urinal too often. Everyone knows there are salesmen who have to maintain an incredible pace of salesmanship, continually driven by their bosses, and that the ones with the lowest sales are automatically discharged, with no excuses accepted. You know about these things. Then you must not object if I put them on screen and satirise them.'

When, around the same time, the world was fast sliding into a systemic crisis, Chaplin couldn't help making a statement that was profound. He said, 'In the new film my Charlie will not be quite so nice. I am sharpening the edge of his character so that people who have liked him vaguely will have to make up their minds.'

Appeared *The Great Dictator* [1940].

5

He stands before the mirror and confronts his double: Devil incarnate ...

In his book *Chaplin: His Life and Art*, David Robinson started his chapter on *The Great Dictator* with these lines: 'Quite apart from any particular merits of the film, *The Great Dictator* remains an unparalleled phenomenon, an epic incident in the history of mankind. The greatest clown and best-loved personality of his age directly challenged the man who had instigated more evil and human misery than any other in modern history.'

The man, of course, was Hitler who, together with his comrades-in-arms, Mussolini in Italy and Tojo in the Far East, not to speak of Franco in Spain earlier, built the Axis Powers to exterminate all that stood for

decency and human compassion. A couple of years back, Rabindranath Tagore [1861 – 1941]—in reply to Japan's national poet Yone Noguchi's [1875 – 1947] defence of Japanese militarism—said clearly and firmly: 'I wish your countrymen, whom I love so much, not success but remorse.' Around the same time, when India was still under British rule, the man who, years later, would become the first Prime Minister of the independent country, Jawaharlal Nehru [1889 – 1964], felt terribly disturbed by the reckless advent of the fascists upon the world. He said that he was sick of the tread of the barbarian feet day after day. Intellectuals all over the world, who looked for life and freedom, reacted sharply to 'the tyranny of collective mediocrity.' And Chaplin was no exception.

That was the time when, in utter desperation, Chaplin rejected the idea of making films with no sound. That was the time when he used words from beginning to end. And after that he never stopped. For such a changeover, he did not offer any apology. On the contrary, emphatically did he say that in the situation the world had been thrown into, he had no choice but to talk—talk unceasingly, talk to the nervous exasperation of those who just could not be summarily dismissed.

The Great Dictator

Nevertheless, questions were raised from different quarters. Those who loved Chaplin's language of pantomime (and who didn't!) were confused. Would Chaplin turn his back on what he had done so wonderfully over these years, all without sound! In his book of essays—*Our Films, Their Films* [1992]—Satyajit Ray, referring to silent films, said, 'Today one can actually question whether the introduction of words into films was not in fact an introduction of an impurity undermining the direct visual impact of the medium. There is no denying the fact that, with the coming of sound, images in films became in general less meaningful in themselves. After all, with sound and with words one can always fall back on speech to convey one's meaning.' Ray added, 'When Chaplin eats his shoes in *The Gold Rush*, he performs an act which is not only funny but is also rich with overtones of symbolic meaning conveyed by purely visual means. A scene like this could never have been conceived in literary terms. And yet when Chaplin himself, in a literary mood, indulges in metaphysical pronouncements in films like *Monsieur Verdoux* and *Limelight*, he conveys less sense in a less purely artistic manner than that single bit of business with the shoe in *The Gold Rush*.'

I, for one, would not agree with Ray's argument regarding films with and without sound. His views on the matter, to my mind, remain universally debatable without, however, leading to any conclusion. But, interestingly, in Ray's newly released selection of essays, *Deep Focus* [2011], he said, 'The point I'm trying to make is that the sound film is not an improvement on the silent film, but an independent art form with its own special appeal and its own special aesthetics. Ideally, the two (forms) should have coexisted.'

Wonderful! In this connection, I am tempted to go back to my own experiences. In my hometown, I still remember being woken up in the morning by the chirping of birds. But, later, in the early forties in Calcutta, I used to be woken up by a peculiar sound—click-clack-clatter—when, early in the morning, the municipality cleaners used long hosepipes from which water rushed out with tremendous force to clean the streets and lanes. That used to be a daily routine in those days. Strangely, I heard (!) the same sound—click-clack-clatter—when in Eisenstein's silent film *The Strike* [1923], ice-cold water was turned in violent fury on the striking workers in order to disperse them. In the absence of sound it was the editing that created the magic. I had a similar experience when

I watched shots of the Czar's soldiers walking down the steps at Odessa in Eisenstein's *Battleship Potemkin* [1925]. Vigorous footsteps were clearly audible because of the perfect editing. And, interestingly, when I saw the same film with sound added to the image of the duty-bound soldiers, there I found the whole sequence overdone. Strangely, such dressing with sound being added to the visuals was done by the high-ups in Soviet Cinema.

Here, out of context, and perhaps going beyond my text, I indulge in pulling out a couple of dozen lines from Jay Leyda's [1910 – 1988] fascinating book *Kino: A History of the Russian and Soviet Film* [1983].

The Canadian Leyda, much older than me, was brilliant, in addition to being a friend of mine.

He went to Moscow to study cinema. His contemporaries included Ivor Montague, a trade union activist from the UK, and Eduard Tisse [1897 – 1961] from Finland. Tisse, later, became Eisenstein's cameraman. All three of them were favourite students of Eisenstein.

On completion of *Battleship Potemkin* Eisenstein realised that Constantin Shvedchikov, the president of the all-powerful studio Sovkino, had reservations about *Potemkin*. And it was well-known that Shvedchikov—an inveterate communist, who had given shelter to Lenin during the October Revolution—was 'slightly anti-Semitic'. In private conversation Shvedchikov used to call Eisenstein 'The nobleman of Jerusalem.'

There were two private screenings of *Battleship Potemkin* for eminent critics and intellectuals, including the outstanding poet, Vladimir Mayakovsky.

After the screening, Mayakovsky was the first to take the floor. He spoke, as usual, in a thunderous voice, pounding the table with his fists and rapping on the floor with the heavy cane he always carried at the time. He knew about Shvedchikov's unfavourable view of the film, and so he demanded that Shvedchikov should immediately export *Potemkin*, saying that he would go down in history as a villain if he did not. Several times Shvedchikov tried to get a word in, but in vain. Having finished his speech, Mayakovsky had turned to go when Shvedchikov asked, 'Are you through? If you are, I would like to say a few words myself.'

Mayakovsky paused at the doorway and replied with great dignity: 'I'm not through yet, and I won't be for at least five hundred years. Shvedchikovs will come and go, but art remains.

Remember that!'

And, as Satyajit Ray rightly said in his essay, and elsewhere too, silent film and talking films are two self-sufficient art forms, distinct in every possible way.Interestingly, in a letter on 26 November 1929, Rabindranath Tagore is reported to have expressed the same idea: 'The primary feature of the silent cinema is the motion of the images. These moving images should be expressed in such a way that the beauty and glory of a sequence can be understood without resorting to the use of words and sentences. If an extraneous language dictates the language of the cinema then it can have a crippling effect on the cinematic language.'

Back to *The Great Dictator.*

In addition to using words and sound in *The Great Dictator* Chaplin played a double role—the role of a Jew barber as an extension of his 'conception of the average man' and the role of a 'Dictator'—Charlie confronting his double, the devil incarnate.

There was a mass rally. The Dictator (Chaplin) was ready for a speech. A smart officer stretched his right arm in salute and said, 'Heil Hynkel!'

As if in a single voice the crowd thundered, 'Heil Hynkel!!!'

The thunder was triumphant and threatening.

The innocent Jew barber (Chaplin) who was busy cutting hair in his shop looked up and asked his friend and assistant, Hannah, 'Who is he?'

Instantly storm-troopers rushed into the barber's modest shop and vandalised it. Hannah was miraculously saved.

Storm-troopers were marching around shouting slogans and carrying messages from the Dictator to terrorise the Jews and the non-Aryans. In the words of the Dictator: 'The rights of citizenship will be taken away from the Jews and other non-Aryans. They are inferior and, therefore, enemies of the State. It is the duty of all true Aryans to hate and despise them.'

Even then, in a busy street, a few protesters shouted slogans defending the democratic right of speech and so on. Storm-troopers kicked up a row.

Amidst all this the Dictator made his speech: '*Democratia shtunk*! (Democracy stinks), *Libertad shtunk* (Liberty is despicable), *Frei sprachen shtunk* (Free speech is objectionable)...' The Dictator said all this and finally, in fury, shouted, '*Tighten der belten* (Gird up your loins)!'

As the Dictator got more and more excited and fiery in his speech, the voice and the words grew confused, and the microphones started crumbling and collapsing, one after another.

The interpreter realised that the crowds were having problems following his speech. So he made it simple for them. He said, 'The speech was all about the Jews.'

The meeting dispersed as planned. The Dictator was in a hurry. He got up and was about to walk out. The officers and the storm-troopers surrounded him. An officer came up and ceremoniously saluted, 'Heil

Hynkel!' The Dictator recognised him as someone who was somehow offensive. He shouted at him, 'Traitor! Democrat!'—the officer was fired.

Then came an ostentatious display of his status through diverse activities, all shown in haste. Photographers and sculptors surrounded the Dictator. He allowed them to do their jobs. A tailor appeared with a bullet-proof long coat, which looked as though made of silk. Wasting no time, he asked the tailor to wear the coat. The tailor immediately obeyed the order and stood confident. An officer offered the Dictator a loaded revolver. The Dictator fired. The tailor fell down, dead. The Dictator said, 'Far from perfect', and walked away to the other room.

Every bit of action was perfect, every shot was faultless, the editing did not allow for a single extra frame. Every sequence was mathematically precise and in perfect rhythm.

Garbitsch and Herring were closest to Dictator. They brought big news—three thousand workers in a big factory were on strike. They asked, 'Should we ... ?'

'Have them all shot,' the Dictator said. He added,

'I do not want any of my workers dissatisfied.'

'Who then will be left to work?' they asked.

Garbitsch looked deep into the Dictator. The Dictator felt a little nervous. Garbitsch said, 'You must not have any doubt that you will be the ultimate ruler of the world.'

Hynkel, a bit uncertain, asked, 'You really mean that?'

Garbitsch said, 'Definitely, you will come to grips with the universe. I mean the whole universe. Yes, indeed, the whole universe.'

Hynkel, still feeling unsure, said, 'What you say scares me at times.'

Behind the camera

Instantly I was reminded of a touching report by the Soviet writer Ilya Ehrenburg [1891 – 1967]. During the holocaust in the early forties of the last century, a large group of Jews, men and women, young and old, were stripped naked in the biting cold; they were huddled together facing a Nazi firing squad. A child, hardly five years old, who did not realise what it was all about, embraced his mother and helplessly said, 'Ma, I am afraid.' Just that, nothing more.

Of course, Dictator Hynkel was not a child, but an arch-criminal and an enemy of the people, but he also felt 'scared' at Garbitsch's prattle!

Garbitsch went on with his gibberish, 'The entire world will fall at your feet.'

'Leave me alone!' The Dictator rushed out.

Alone in the other room, the Dictator felt defenceless. He looked at the globe on the table.

Next appeared on the screen that unforgettable scene from *The Great Dictator*—Hynkel playing with 'the terrestrial globe'. In a trance, the Dictator played savagely, laughed gustily, danced furiously, bounced the globe from wrist to wrist and off the top of his head, even back-kicked it away viciously, all intensely Chaplinesque, all caught in perfect rhythm. Thus the world floated into his hands, bounced on his buttocks and back to his greedy hands. Suddenly the globe popped.

Returning to himself, the Dictator was back at his job.

Charlie, the Jew barber, and his friend Hannah together outsmarted the storm-troopers and ran away. Hannah said, 'Never mind, we can start over again in Austerlich.'

Without giving the Dictator a moment's rest, Garbitsch brought the news that Benzino Napaloni, the Dictator of Bacteria, had stationed an army, sixty thousand strong, at the border of Austerlich. The Dictator Hynkel got furious and asked Garbitsch to immediately organise a meeting with Napaloni.

The meeting was a funny game, very soberly staged, where both the Dictators tried to prove their superiority and authority. Eventually, Napaloni had no alternative but to withdraw his armed forces, and Hynkel got ready to attack Austerlich.

Even as Hannah and Charlie found a safe shelter in Austerlich along with an old Jew, Hynkel crossed the border with his well-disciplined army. Surprisingly, there was no counter-attack and their victory was clean and simple.

Advised by Garbitsch and Herring, the Dictator went into hiding as a precautionary measure.

A mammoth meeting was organised to celebrate the victory, where the 'future emperor of the world' was to make an appropriate speech. But the Dictator was hiding and could not be traced. A desperate search and a fierce combing operation by the storm-troopers brought the man to address the vanquished people of Austerlich. The powers-that-be implored him to speak a few words. The man was none other than the Jew barber—the resemblance, though remarkable, being purely coincidental.

Charlie, the Jew barber, looked around helplessly. Once again his name was announced as the 'future emperor of the world'. Charlie stood up, still a bit nervous, and started to speak. He spoke: 'I am sorry, but I do not want to be an emperor. This is not my business ... I should like to help everybody if possible—Jew, gentile, black, white ... Life can be free and beautiful, but we have lost the way. Greed has poisoned men's souls.'

Elsewhere Hannah, distressed and yet hopeful, was listening to Charlie, the Jew barber, as he began to speak.

Slowly but steadily Charlie started growing, growing beyond himself, and finally made his speech, a long speech, very long, six-minutes' duration, something which, in the history of world cinema, no one had ever heard before.

Charlie said: 'The hate will pass, and Dictators will die, and the power they took from the people will return to the people. The aeroplane and the radio have brought us closer together. The very nature of these inventions cries out for the goodness in man, cries out for universal brotherhood, for the unity of us all … . Soldiers! Do not give yourselves to these brutes—men who despise you, enslave you, regiment your lives, treat you like cattle and use you as cannon-fodder. You are not machines. You are men! You have the love of humanity in your heart. Soldiers! Do not fight for slavery. Fight for liberty. You, the people, have the power, the power to create machines, the power to create happiness. You people have the power to make this life free and beautiful, to make this life a wonderful adventure ...'

Charlie Chaplin's 'concept of the average man' shone through: 'The clouds are lifting, the sun is breaking through, we are coming out of the darkness into a new world where men will rise above their hate, their greed and their brutality. The soul of man has been given wings and at last he is beginning to fly. He is flying into the rainbow, into the light of hope, into the future, into the glorious future that belongs to you, to me, and to all of us.'

The crowd—the vanquished, the oppressed,

the dispossessed, and, of course, Hannah and the unknown old Jew accompanying her—all listened to the speech spellbound. They were overwhelmed.

The unnamed old Jew said, 'Do you hear?'

'Hush!' she said.

Hannah was in tears. She looked divine.

The film created a stir when it was released. It was loved by almost everyone. They considered the film great. Some had questions, some had problems, and a few got furious. Chaplin had to make a statement about his intentions. He said, 'I wanted to see the return of decency and kindness. I am no communist ... I am just a human being who wants to see this country as a real democracy with freedom from this infernal regimentation which is crawling over the rest of the world.'

In another statement, he said, 'It would be much easier to have the barber and Hannah disappear over the horizon, off to a promised land against the glowing sunset. But there is no promised land for the oppressed people of the world. There is no place over the horizon to which they can go for sanctuary. They must stand and so must we.'

There followed quite a few political statements which, because of his sense of urgency, he felt confident about issuing. He sent a message to a big rally in New York and categorically said that real democracy could be rightly restored in the Russian battlefield. And he openly urged the concerned authorities to open a Second Front on the Western Frontier in Europe. When there was a conspiracy to throw the world-famous communist music composer Hans Eisler [1898 – 1962] out of America, he sent a cable to Pablo Picasso [1881 – 1973] to protest against the heinous plan and organise a popular protest all over Europe.

Dangerously active, the Un-American Activities Committee built a nasty campaign against Chaplin. To which he quietly said, 'I am no communist, I am all for peace to settle on earth.'

'How is it that you are still an *outsider*, and not a citizen of America?' fumed the Un-American Activities Committee.

Chaplin's was a forthright reply, quiet and firm, 'I am a citizen of the world. I am an internationalist, not a nationalist, and that is why I do not take citizenship.'

That was when he wrote, for a periodical, 'Before long, I shall perhaps leave the United States, although it has given me so many moral and material satisfactions. I, Charlie Chaplin, declare that Hollywood is dying, that Hollywood is fighting its last battle, and it will lose that battle unless it decides, once and for all, to give up standardising its films, unless it realises that masterpieces cannot be mass-produced in the cinema, like tractors in a factory.'

Around that time, when Chaplin was attacked from all sides for being 'antisocial and a communist', he married for the fourth time the famous playwright Eugene O'Neill's [1888 – 1953] eighteen-year-old daughter, Oona. Chaplin was fifty-four.

The War in Europe came to an official end in late April 1945, but the storm was still raging. There was no sign of peace on the world scene.

Perhaps recalling Romain Rolland's [1866 – 1944] *I Will Not Rest*, Chaplin got all set for his next film. But for reasons beyond his control, the shooting of *Monsieur Verdoux* started only in April 1946.

Eugene O'Neill

True, although the truce was signed and sealed by the Axis Powers, and Hitler, while hiding in an underground cellar, reportedly committed suicide, and Mussolini's dead body was dragged out by his own people in the middle of what was once a busy thoroughfare, for the people to see and spit on, there was no peace anywhere. And, unbelievably, four months later, in August 1945, Hiroshima and Nagasaki in Japan were devastated by the American Air Force.

Incidentally, thirty-four years later, on an invitation by the Japanese Government for a fortnight's visit in Japan, I went there for the first time. On being allowed to chalk out my own programme, my first choice was to go to Hiroshima.

On 18 March 1979, I reached Hiroshima via Kyoto and Nara, the ancient capital of Japan, with my friend Akira Iwasaki [1903 – 1981]. Akira was a film historian and the author of a brilliant book on Hiroshima and Nagasaki with rare photographs and illustrations. I was told later on that he died of cancer.

Anyway, Akira and I came to the museum gate of the sprawling ruins. Akira took me to a particular spot and stopped. What a sight! In breathtaking silence, I stood with my eyes riveted to the gruesome past of Hiroshima-Nagasaki, staring at the face of a boy, larger than life, silent and static, eyes bearing an awful vacuity and horror. The boy, now turned into an image, stood with a rice-ball in his hand.

Akira, standing beside me, said that he was just one of the nameless segment of humanity that witnessed hell before their eyes. He too must have succumbed to radiation, may be not that day, may be a couple of days later, may be a long time later. Who knows—perhaps he was one of the survivors, put in strict quarantine in a special hospital in Hiroshima, one of those who still carried within themselves the grisly memory of that day. Now, standing before the boy with a rice-ball in his hand, I saw history embodied, a history that I could follow to those days when the whole of humanity witnessed the reckless nuclear holocaust unleashed upon the world.

On our return to the hotel, Akira gave me an audio-cassette, and I borrowed a tape recorder from the hotel reception. After dinner, I retired to my room, and Akira to his. Alone in my room, I listened to the tape: ' ... None of the Allied partners was taken into confidence about the horror that was going to be perpetrated within the next few days. As a matter of fact, may be to camouflage the operation, the US Air Force dropped anti-war leaflets over Hiroshima and a few neighbouring cities for some days at a stretch, before the three bomber airplanes appeared in the clear sky above Hiroshima early morning on 6 August. Without any warning whatsoever, one of the planes zoomed down on the city, and in a moment disappeared into the western sky. That was in 1945, on 6 August, at 08:15 hours, Hiroshima time.'

'It had taken just a moment: the sky broke into flames, followed by a terrible blast, and in ten minutes, a fire shot through the whole city, heat sizzling red-hot, temperatures shooting up between 2000 and 7000 degrees centigrade, turning the

Nagasaki, 1945

neighbourhood into a burnt-out wilderness. Running flames, a sheet of blazing heat and an unbearable force of wind rushed through the city, tearing it down, shattering it to shards, burning it to the skies, wiping it away from the face of the earth in a moment. Then came rain, dark and sinister ...

'Three days later, on 9 August 1945, Nagasaki fell in the same manner to yet another bomb—both barely three metres in length, weighing four tons each ...'

Next morning I asked Akira what, when the war was virtually over, was the need for such a mass-killing operation; and why, of all choices of weaponry, the nuclear bomb? War or no war, had anybody heard of dropping an atom bomb, ever? Those were the basic questions fermenting within Akira Iwasaki too. He did not expect an answer from me, he did not need it. He had the answer: 'American hegemony! What else?'

6

Depression and War: Floating a business

Chaplin found himself busy with a hundred things that he could not ignore. Jotting and scribbling, crumpling up half-formed thoughts, tossing them away, he finally started leafing through his diary, picking out entries—trivial, personal—and making important notes. Without ever going into hibernation, he got into planning, drafting, writing a new film which was later shelved. And all the time he was doggedly engaged in organising a campaign for the opening of a Second Front to resist the Nazis as they attacked the Soviet Union. He knew very well that, despite the alliance between the Allied Powers to fight Hitler's army, there were widespread anti-Soviet feelings amongst a large number of Americans who were quite happy to see mounting Russian casualties on the Eastern Front. It was simple arithmetic for Chaplin to realise that the confrontation on the Eastern Front would produce the mutual destruction of both Nazis and communists.

World War II was one of the bloodiest battles in history, and admittedly, the deadliest of all was the Battle of Stalingrad. That was in 1942 when a massive chunk of Hitler's army was pulled out of Western Front and rushed to Stalingrad to thoroughly shatter the city and the surroundings. The besieged people braved the invaders and fought them in the streets and alleys, from building to building, from door to door, from window to window. The total casualty, Russians and Germans out together, rose up to a staggering figure of around two million!!!

Chaplin received a telephone call from the American Committee for Russian War Relief. He readily accepted their invitation. When he arrived in San Francisco he saw a crowd of around ten thousand people listening to the speakers. When Chaplin's turn came, he addressed the crowd as 'Comrades'! He said, 'I assume there are many Russians here tonight, and the way your countrymen are fighting and dying at the moment, it is an honour and a privilege to call you comrades.'

Instant enthusiasm from the audience spurred

Chaplin to freely speak his mind. Once again, he said, 'I am no communist, but a human being, and I think I know the reactions of human beings.' He continued, 'The communists are no different from anyone else; whether they lose an arm or a leg, they suffer as all of us do, and die as all of us die.'

At this moment, suddenly, remaining contemporary and sounding like a Shakespearean actor (with shades of *The Merchant of Venice*), he said, 'And a communist mother is the same as any other mother. When she receives the tragic news that her son will not return, she weeps as other mothers weep. I, Charlie Chaplin, do not have to be a communist to know that. And, at this moment, Russian mothers are doing a lot of weeping and their sons a lot of dying.'

Chaplin called upon the enthusiastic crowd to send ten thousand telegrams to President Roosevelt [1882–1945] demanding the opening of a Second Front in Europe.

According to Chaplin's colleagues, and to some of the stalwarts in the world of cinema, his was a tremendous speech. It was a bold political stand to take at that time.

Two months after the San Francisco speech, he was requested to address a mass rally at Madison Square. Chaplin prepared a speech for radio-telephone and read it out. Again, he called for a Second Front. He concluded, 'Let us aim for victory in the Spring. You in the factories, you in the fields, you in uniforms, you the citizens of the world, let us work and fight towards that end. You, official Washington, and you, official London, let us make this our aim—victory in the Spring!'

For such speeches and many more such appeals, in America, England, everywhere, Chaplin, as usual, was bombarded with bouquets and brickbats—both. He remained firm and resolute.

Enough! Now, to his next film.

Orson Welles [1915–1985] came to Chaplin with a proposal. He was planning to make a documentary on the career of Landru, the notorious French wife-murderer. It was still unscripted. Orson Welles wanted Chaplin to play the principal role. After a few days, Chaplin telephoned Welles to say that his suggestion, though not yet written, had given him a new idea for a comedy. That was about all the talk they had, and that was how Chaplin started planning his next script. Called *Monsieur Verdoux*, it had absolutely no connection with the real-life Landru.

Now, with the idea popping into his head, Chaplin watched the state of affairs in the world, like the blatant atrocity perpetrated on Hiroshima-Nagasaki. He stopped awhile, grew desperate, threw a challenge at everything that came his way. He decided that his Charlie would toss away his bowler hat, fling off his buttoned coat, and trim his moustache; yet his persona would remain unchanged, his manners more or less the same. On the surface, he looked like a mere commoner, Monsieur Verdoux by name, who grabbed the job of a clerk in a metropolitan bank in France. Soon after, when the Stock Exchange was in panic and the year [1929] of the Depression was in the offing, he received with his pay packet a notice of dismissal. In the lean years that followed, when millionaires faced bad times and worse, Verdoux had to keep himself going, along with his wife and child. His disabled wife and his only child, Peter, both living in an untroubled village, were all that he had on this earth. And they were his dependants.

Verdoux floated a business of his own—the business of killing. Indiscriminately, regardless of age, he began to play lover to an assortment of wealthy women—a sort of a sport with fatal consequences for all other players, because his 'business' was to kill them off, one by one, and grab their wealth. A ruthless business! But isn't all business ruthless?

Defending Vardoux's ruthless business, Chaplin stated: 'The picture has moral values, I believe. Von Clausewitz said that war is the logical extension of diplomacy. M. Verdoux feels that murder is the logical extension of business. He should express the feeling of the time we live in. Out of catastrophe come people like him. He typifies the psychological disease and depression. He is frustrated, bitter, and, at the end, pessimistic.

'But he is never morbid; and the picture is by no means morbid in treatment ... Under the proper circumstances, murder can be comic.'

So, in *Monsieur Verdoux*, murder was a sort of comical exercise, and when the people watched a murder they did not hold their breath, they did not have to. They laughed and laughed and laughed.

And not just one murder; Verdoux finished off a dozen women of high social standing. To give just one example, one of the women came to Verdoux with an important assignment and introduced herself as the widow of an affluent man. Immediately, the idea of business popped into his head. He led her to his bedroom, and said that he and his dear wife had lived together for many years until she suddenly died. The woman, now middle-aged, felt sorry for Verdoux. Coming close to her and looking deep into her eyes, he said: 'Your eyes are deep pools of desire.' When the middle-aged woman resisted, the insistent Verdoux implored, 'Nonsense! What difference does age make? You have ripeness, luxuriousness, more experience, more character now, more everything ...'. And he embraced her. Nothing happened at the time, but it worked later ... . A difficult job, difficult and cumbersome! And ruthless, of course, like all business.

Verdoux was always in a mad hurry. He suddenly arrived in his village and gave his wife a big surprise. He brought gifts for his wife and son. He asked her to remember their wonderful years together. It was their marriage anniversary. Verdoux confessed to his wife: 'These are desperate days. Millions are starving and unemployed. It is not easy for a man of my age.'

Verdoux watched his son pulling the tail of his cat. The cat mewed in protest. Verdoux rebuked the boy gently and said: 'There is a cruel streak in you. I wonder where you get it from. Remember, violence begets violence.'

Verdoux had no time to waste. On his way to Paris, he saw a friend of his, an experienced chemist. Innocently, and with excitement, he told Verdoux that he had invented a powder that, if consumed, would kill a person immediately, leaving no trace of poison in the body. Verdoux asked for a sample. The chemist obligingly gave him a small packet. He smiled and the chemist smiled back.

Late in the evening Verdoux reached Paris. In the freezing cold he saw a young woman sitting on the pavement. She looked upset and troubled. He felt sad, picked her up and took her to his apartment.

Verdoux quickly started preparing a meal for the young woman. She was touched by his warmth and kindness. She told him all about herself. She said that

Monsieur Verdoux

her husband had returned from the Front severely wounded and died soon after. Her memories of her days with her dear husband helped her survive even through her darkest hours.

Verdoux listened while pouring a drink for her, and smiled sceptically. The young woman could read his unspoken disbelief. Mildly she scolded him, 'How little you know about women!'

While mixing the chemist's powder with her drink, Verdoux looked at her and, a bit shaken, changed his mind, offered her another glass without powder. A broad smile flashing across his face, he said, with perfect ease: 'Your philosophy may corrupt me.'

Despite such unwanted interruptions, Verdoux continued his business as usual and eventually killed a dozen women.

Suddenly a short collage flashed on the screen—a series of shots, related and unrelated, including some contemporary newsreel coverage which had never appeared before in any of Chaplin's earlier films, long or short. The collage was a cruel revelation of the sorry state of affairs in the troubled society. In the midst of all this, Verdoux was seen coming out of a hotel, dreadfully crushed and lonely. He seemed to be on the verge of a nervous breakdown. It was late in the evening. He walked through the crowd. Paris looked like an infernal city, unredeemed and doomed.

An expensive cab was seen making its way through the crowd. A sweet voice was heard from inside the cab: 'Hey!'

It was a gentle exclamation. Verdoux looked back and walked a few shaky steps. 'Ah, it is you!' he said, a bit surprised.

'So, you recognise me!' the girl said, 'I am the same woman whom you saved from the freezing cold. I

Monsieur Verdoux

still remember you for all that you did for me that night.'

Verdoux said, 'Forget it. But how come you are here?' He was looking at the cab.

'I am now the mistress of a munitions manufacturer.' she said proudly.

Verdoux nodded, and said, 'I see! I made a mistake in my life. I should have taken to the profession of your friend.'

Verdoux made a move, but stopped when she asked, 'Where are you going?'

'I am going to meet my destiny.'

He made himself scarce.

Then, Verdoux, on being arrested, faced the inquisitors. He had nothing to fear. He knew very well that he, on his own, had come to meet his destiny.

The inquisitors sat in judgement. They charged the dismissed bank clerk with cold-blooded mass-murder. They condemned him to death.

Keeping his cool Verdoux said in a no-nonsense manner: 'Mass-murder! Doesn't the world encourage it? I am an amateur in comparison.' He continued, 'Murder is the logical extension of business. And all business is ruthless business.'

Before leaving the court surrounded by guards, he cast a casual glance at the inquisitors, saying, 'I'll see you all soon, very soon.'

In the prison cell the priest came to the condemned man, produced a pocket edition of the Holy Bible and asked for a confession. Quietly Verdoux said: 'I have no conflict with God; my conflict is with man.'

A high-up member of the Crime-Does-Not-Pay-Society came to him and wanted him to admit that crime could never pay. He said: 'Not in a small way. One murder makes a villain, millions a hero. Numbers sanctify.'

Just before his execution Verdoux was offered rum to drink. He thanked them, and declined, but then immediately said: 'Just a minute, I have never tasted rum.' He gulped it down.

Verdoux came out into the open, looked around. And he drew a deep breath.

Monsieur Verdoux

Venice Film Festival, 1972. My film *Calcutta 71* was the only entry from India. There were twenty more films from all over the world for the main section. I was invited to present my film at the festival, which I did. But I spent most of my time during the two-week-long festival, from morning till midnight, everyday, watching a fabulous event in another section, called *Il Tutto Chaplin* (The Whole of Chaplin), which, in a way, made me feel wiser than before. It was a brilliant exercise for my greater understanding of the great comedian. When the festival was over I made a short detour to Milan on my way back to India.

In Milan I had to take part in a seminar on Chaplin. I was asked how I reacted to the maestro's total rejection of his Charlie persona and his turning into a new character in *Monsieur Verdoux*.

To be honest to myself, I had to say, 'I am afraid I do not agree with you. Vis-à-vis the context in which Verdoux was presented to me and the world audience, he was not an unknown character. He was the logical extension of Chaplin's earlier character—"Charlie". Instead of pointing the finger at the millionaire—an individual—Verdoux fired directly at the class—the class which believed in mass murder: war—or holocaust, for that matter. A simple equation is using Chaplin's statement:

"Murder is the logical extension of business." And, again, Chaplin said: "Under the proper circumstances, murder can be comic." People's reaction is no different, it is the same with Charlie, as with Verdoux—laughter.'

In Milan, some agreed with me and the rest did not. But I have never been scared of controversies. Not till today. As the great physicist Niels Bohr once said: 'Truth attains a quality only when it becomes controversial.'

7

Old wine in a new bottle: An ageing Chaplin creates Calvero in *Limelight*

Immediately after the release of *Monsieur Verdoux*, the debate, as always, grew intense. Opinions were sharply divided. People either loved the film or hated it. The committee of Catholic War Veterans attacked Chaplin endlessly. The Un-American Activities Committee made his stay in America almost impossible. Chaplin fought them fiercely without budging an inch, and then, looking into himself, thought about his new film. He said, 'In these days of hate and suspicion I am now trying to say something about human kindness.'

When Chaplin defended the famous music composer Hans Eisler, and organised a huge campaign to fight against his unfortunate extradition, the Committee asked a particular journalist of repute to attack him in the strongest possible manner. This man, Westbrook Pegler [1894–1969], referring to

Chaplin's support for Eisler, wrote savagely: 'This was an attempt by an alien, resident here for more than thirty-five years, guilty of a degree of moral turpitude which disqualifies him from citizenship, caught in the act of cheating the government of an enormous debt for taxes, a slacker in both World Wars, although he clamoured with the communists for a Second Front in the latest one.'

Brushing it all aside, Chaplin launched into his new project *Limelight* [1952].

Initially, Chaplin wrote it as a piece of short fiction, but afterwards rewrote it as a script. It was about an ageing music hall comedian, Calvero by name, who started feeling that he was fast losing his spirit and self-confidence as he grew older. Sadly, he decided that the 'comic Muse' had left him. He came in contact with a young dancer, Terry, who was also very unsure of herself. To cut a long story short, the ageing comedian and the young dancer built a world of their own. Calvero gave a brilliant performance on stage, after which, exhausted, he almost collapsed in the wings. He saw Terry, on stage, still continuing to dance gracefully, and declared, 'I must go on .... That is progress.'

The ending, unlike in any of Chaplin's previous films, looked and sounded rather sentimental. To my mind and perhaps to everyone's, *Limelight* was to some extent autobiographical.

I recall that at the 1989 Venice Film Festival, when my Film *Ekdin Achanak* (Suddenly One Day) was presented, a critic asked me, 'To what extent is your film autobiographical?' I smiled. I looked into myself, smiled again, and said, 'To the extent it is yours.' I thought I gave a simple answer to a simple question, even though I recognised that it was not the right answer for everyone. Later, in the 1989 London Film Festival, Derek Malcolm of *The Guardian* wrote:

'Sen's portrait of the self-doubting protagonist (a retired professor) is fascinating, since it is clearly intended to be autobiographical, and a discourse about success and failure that is as frank and honest as anything Sen has yet put on the screen ... and he sums up the Calcutta ambience with a masterly eye for detail.'

The remarkable details, from beginning to end, were what I loved so much in Chaplin's *Limelight*.

Limelight could well be seen as a family reunion, as his children, including Geraldine (Oona's eldest daughter), and probably even Chaplin's step-brother Sydney, all acted in it. Besides, most importantly of all, two of the greatest comedians of the silent era, Buster Keaton [1895–1966] and Chaplin, appeared together for the first time. That was a stupendous sight.

Perhaps Chaplin's longest film, *Limelight* was premiered simultaneously in New York and London on 23 October 1952. Chaplin's decision was to attend the London premiere along with his children and Oona in particular. This was Oona's first trip to London.

During the journey by ship Chaplin came to know about the legal procedures to block his re-entry to America. The U.S. Attorney General, James McGranery, had rescinded his re-entry permit and ordered the Immigration Services to bar him pending an enquiry. Further news regarding his case was unknown.

When, a few days later, his ship docked, a number of journalists and story-builders bombarded Chaplin with their stock-phrases to which Chaplin simply answered: 'I have not come here to become an international crisis ... I do not want to create any revolution. All I want to do is to make a few more films. Such films might amuse people. I hope so ... I've never been political. I have no political convictions. I'm an individualist, and I believe in liberty.'

Chaplin, his family and his team reached London. He felt greatly pleased. As the head of the family it was a matter of great satisfaction to him.

After the premiere in London, the film was shown in Paris. Aragon, Picasso, Jean-Paul Sartre and other cultural and intellectual stalwarts formed a colourful gathering. Prominently missing was the American Ambassador who, it was very clear, was not invited.

The response, however, was mixed. Most of the people enjoyed the film, but there were quite a few who had reservations. Picasso, for instance, gave his candid opinion rather strongly. He said: 'The real tragedy lies in the fact that Chaplin can no longer assume the physical appearance of the clown because he is no longer slender, no longer young, and no longer has the face and the expression of his "little man", but that of a man who had grown old. His body is not really him any more. Time has conquered him and turned him into another person. And now he is a lost soul—just another actor in search of his individuality, and he won't be able to make anybody laugh.'

Chaplin was not a man to hibernate. Ideas kept popping into his head. And the one that came to the forefront was an idea about a displaced person arriving in the New World. The person he was creating was to have an accident while travelling. He would get sick in the head. He would lose his speech. He would mutter a new language which no one could follow. The officers at the Immigration Counter would have problems with him. He would start gesticulating, miming—which he could do efficiently. Having absolutely no clue as to how to deal with his case, the authorities would allow the immigrant to finally cross the barrier. The rest was a *A King in New York* [1957]. Not an American movie, but a British production.

Meanwhile, event after event continued to unfold, and statements and counter-statements followed one after another. At last, in utter despair and disgust, Chaplin decided to pull up his roots in America.

He sold off his studio and properties at throw-away prices, signed and sealed the deals, and issued a public statement. He said: 'I have been the object of lies and vicious propaganda by powerful reactionary groups who, by their influence and aided by America's yellow press, have created an unhealthy atmosphere in which liberal—minded individuals can be singled out and persecuted. Under these conditions I find it virtually impossible to continue my motion picture work, and I have, therefore, given up my residence in the United States.'

Without waiting for the official order, Chaplin decided not to return to America ever again.

Now, returning to his project, with the title remaining unchanged, *A King in New York*, Chaplin redrafted the body of the text in which, based closely on his own experiences, he sharply satirised the activities of the FBI and the Un-American Activities Committee.

The script began with a sub-title: 'One of the minor annoyances of modern life is a *revolution*.' The exiled King Shahdov of Estrovia sought refuge in the United States where he hoped to pursue his plans regarding the peaceful uses of atomic energy. Unfortunately, his corrupt Prime Minister absconded with the funds that were to have financed these plans. The aborted plans notwithstanding, the exiled King visited a progressive school where he met a precocious boy who read Marx and assaulted the king with a rhetorical speech. On a bitter winter night, in a desolate road, the King again met the boy, now homeless. He had run away from school to escape the House Committee on Un-American Activities which wanted to question him about his parents' political loyalties. The FBI took the boy away, and the King himself was called before the Committee. All ended in a fiasco. The exiled King managed to get entangled with a fire hose in typical Chaplinesque manner, and to soak the Committee with water. Finally, he decided to leave America. Before he left the country, he met the boy again and found the once-spirited boy cowed and defeated.

Disjointed situations performed in a slapstick manner were built up to ridiculous McCarthyism.

The reviews were sharply mixed. The celebrated dramatist John Osborne [1929–1994], who wrote the famous play *Look Back in Anger* [1956], made a clear statement. He said: 'In some ways *A King in New York* must be Chaplin's most bitter film ... It goes fairly wide ... some of it is well aimed, some is not. ...'

Chaplin, as usual, had the American press barred from the premiere. His most loyal supporter, Gene Moskowitz [1921 – 1982] of *Variety*, an American periodical, one of the best-loved critics in the world, sadly commented: 'For a man demanding liberty and freedom of expression for himself, it is a negative action.'

Charles Chaplin's next and final film was *A Countess from Hong Kong* [1967]. The film was clearly a popular failure. Even those who liked the film were not

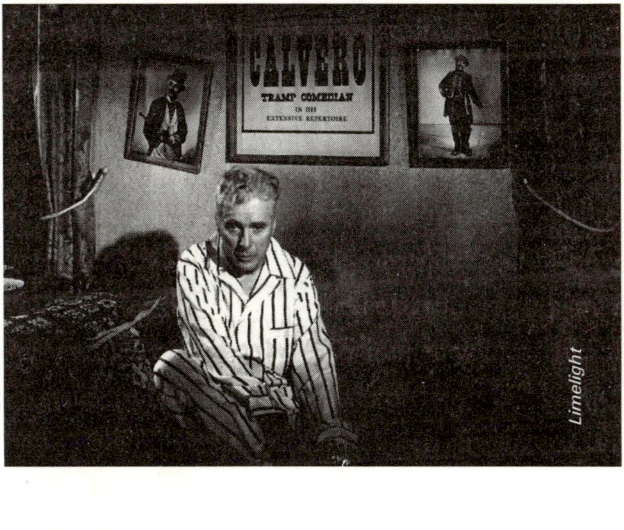

Limelight

Moskowitz was a dear friend of my wife and mine. When, in 1982, I was in the middle of my production *Kharij* (The Case Is Closed), shooting in a Calcutta studio, Moskowitz and a few of our common friends who were attending an international film festival in the city, visited the studio and saw me at work. As they were about to leave, Moskowitz took me aside and said in whisper, 'Mrinal, I can smell a good film.' The following year, when the film was screened in the 1983 Cannes Festival, one notable absentee was Gene Moskowitz. He had died of cancer two months earlier. My European agent and I decided that I should dedicate the film to him. It was done hurriedly, at the festival site, before the screening. Just one line appeared on the screen in the beginning: 'In Memory of Gene Moskowitz'. The film was shown at the press screening in Cannes, with more than seven hundred delegates in the hall. The moment his name appeared on the screen, the entire hall stood up in silence and remained standing until the credits started rolling. My agent and friend Eliane Stutterheim and I were overwhelmed.

enthusiastic about it. And those who did not like it were openly furious. Bosley Crowther [1905 – 1981] of *The New York Times*, a very powerful critic who was famous for making or breaking a film, said, 'Alas, it is a far cry from the great films that Chaplin made, even as late as *Monsieur Verdoux* and *Limelight*, to the painfully antique bedroom farce he put together in *A Countess from Hong Kong* which opened for a continuous run at the Sutton. And if an old fan of Mr Chaplin's movies could have his charitable way, he would draw the curtain fast on this embarrassment and pretend it never occurred. But that cannot be. We have to face it, not only because it has two such answerable performers as Sophia Loren and Marlon Brando in the leading roles, but also because Mr Chaplin has indicated his great pride in it, and because it is being presented with splashy éclat ... .'

Even if we ignore Crowther's review of *A Countess from Hong Kong*, the fact remains that near-eighty Chaplin's last film was much less important than his total achievements during his unforgettable career and throughout his stupendous journey since 1914.

Incidentally, in connection with Bosley Crowther's unkind, even unhealthy, diatribes, let me just say that, watching Satyajit Ray's *Pather Panchali*, an all-time classic, he said that 'the film was of loose structure and had a listless tempo ... It is a film that takes patience to be enjoyed.'

Crowther was the man who kept shouting that he could 'destroy' a film with his pen!

However, he changed his opinion just five days later. His reappraisal about *Pather Panchali* appeared five days later when he wrote: 'It is a cinema mosaic done by an inexperienced man whose priceless assets are integrity, compassion and a great feeling for pictorial imagery ...'

The Idol and the doll

Let us turn to the event when she came to my tiny apartment in 2010. Kiera Chaplin, Chairperson of Limelight Films, and daughter of Eugene Chaplin [b.1953]—Oona's fifth son—accompanied by a local press photographer. She came to see me. She was very much in the news, as the local dailies informed us that Chaplin's granddaughter was in town. From what I gathered, she was here to act in a film being made by an Indian woman director living in Los Angeles. I had received a request that she wanted to come and see me. She came in and her eyes went immediately to the large image of Charlie, the vagabond, mounted on the wall.

Kiera giggled and asked me, 'For me?'

I said, 'For me and for anybody who comes here.'

After a short pause, I said, 'He is for the world and will remain so for eternity.'

8

Chaplin at international film fests—and I

I

Cannes, 1981. Like every other time, this year too the festival was abuzz with excitement. Every day there were films—competition entries—to be watched. Two or three films a day. We, the jury members, had to sign our names in the register before each screening as proof of having actually been present. Along with eight others, among them Gabriel Garcia Marquez, Sydney Lumet and Geraldine Chaplin, I watched the films, attended frequent meetings of the jury, exchanged opinions with the rest. There were some films that we set aside while others we lauded to great heights. Shortlisting, just that. And there were some about which we simply made some conciliatory noises before, again, setting them aside. Having done all this watching and rewatching, we would go back to the hotel to rest.

One day, after watching a film, three of us stepped out—my wife, Geraldine, and I. We strolled down to a restaurant on the beach. Geraldine had already warned me in advance, 'No film talk. Anything but.'

We talked of a few things for a while. Very naturally, the thought of Chaplin occupied the greater part of our minds. At one point, I brought it up. I asked Geraldine, 'Do you remember that story? The story about the Civil War in Spain in 1938?'

Geraldine looked questioningly at me: 'Civil War!'

'Yes, a great story. The moment I read it, I translated it into my own language—Bengali.'

Geraldine probed, 'A story by my father! Written by him! Where did you get it?'

As a matter of fact, I did not find it easily. This original text by Chaplin did not feature in any book on him that I could lay my hands on. I was told that a French translation of the story was available, titled *Rhythme*. I ransacked the National Library in Calcutta, and at last I found the much sought-after story in English in a Chaplin book I had never read before. I devoured it immediately. I was thrilled.

Geraldine really had no idea about its existence. I was surprised. The very same daughter had, just a few years ago, left no stone unturned to help track down the coffin with her father's body which had been stolen from the quiet cemetery in the Swiss village, Vevey, where he was buried, and finally managed to excavate it from a cornfield beside Lake Geneva.

Reportedly, the two young men who committed this stupid crime were later arrested, and the Swiss Court found them guilty and imprisoned them for 'disturbing the peace of the dead.'

I felt an urge to narrate the short story to Geraldine. I recounted most of it exactly the way in which it had been put down by Chaplin. I knew it almost by heart.

The story, called *Rhythm*, had a subtitle: 'The story of men in a macabre movement.'

I made an attempt at ad-lib storytelling. I was not at all happy with it—in fact, it was unfair on my part. But Geraldine was moved, her eyes glistened.

However, the original I discovered at the National Library ran as follows:

> The outskirts of Madrid. A prison. A courtyard at the back. Surrounded by high walls. A Loyalist (anti-Franco) stands at one end of the courtyard. Opposite

to him is the firing squad. Six soldiers. Beside them, the squad leader. The officer in command. Standing some distance away from them is a small group of officers. Waiting eagerly to witness the execution. Everything is as quiet and as still as death itself. The day begins to dawn slowly.

One still believes that things may just turn out differently. At the last moment the powers-that-be will withdraw the death sentence, grant a reprieve. No matter that he is an Oppositionist, a Loyalist, anti-Franco. In reality he is no ordinary person. He is a famous man, known to everybody. The topmost writer of funny stories, he is also an old friend of the squad leader. They have grown up together, studied together, spent time together, chatting. They have spent day after day arguing, fighting, debating. There have been differences of opinion, even mutual conflict with regard to the politics of the country. The same political fight that has today assumed terrifying proportions and is now manifesting itself in the Civil War. They are standing face to face. Between the walls of this prison courtyard.

Memories of their past come back to the officer. But what is the point of remembering? Today, there is no place for arguments and debates. The war has made it all futile. The past is null and void, the friendship is annulled and only the future stares them in the

face. The same future that has provoked the country to act.
The two friends have met today. In this terrible morning. There is silence all around. They look at each other, they smile at each other. Not a word. The morning light slowly spreads over the courtyard.
The rhythm of silence. Almost like the beating of one's heart. And every single person is trapped in that rhythm. The firing squad, the squad leader, everyone.
The squad leader's voice breaks the silence: 'Attention!'
Six rifles shift into places. Six soldiers tighten their grips on their rifles. Strong. Firm. The firing squad tuned to that rhythm.
Unknowingly, something occurs. The young Loyalist coughs slightly. He coughs and clears his throat. Just that.
The rhythm is broken. The beat falters.
The squad leader is hurled aside. Flung away. Trying to clutch at something that floats away from him. He looks at the prisoner.
The prisoner, the young Loyalist, stands still. His back to the wall.
The firing squad? The leader looks towards them. The soldiers seem set to an unyielding time.
The squad leader loses 'consciousness'. He needs

support, looks around. He sees a man standing with his back to the wall. Six soldiers stand facing him. A few more people, a short distance away, wait to see the end. As though a clock had been ticking through eternity, and now the ticking has petered out and dies into silence.

A few inert moments pass by, thus.

Consciousness returns ever so slowly. The squad leader realises he has just given an order. He now comes to grips with himself. He yells to the best of his ability: 'Shoulder arms!'

The soldiers are caught up in the rhythm. They do as required. That restores the rhythm in the leader once again. He yells: 'To aim!'

The six soldiers are ready. Fingers on the triggers. Waiting for the last command.

Just then, footsteps break the silence. People seen to be running in their direction. Has the sentence been repealed, then? Finally, have the powers-that-be paused to change their minds?

In utter desperation, the leader screams: 'Stop!'

Six men wait poised with rifles.

Six men caught in rhythm.

Six men, when they hear the scream to stop, 'Fire!'

A short story. A mere fragment. But possessed of a terrible horror, of an incredible helplessness, reminding one of Dostoevsky facing the Russian firing squad in the Czar's time. Unforgettable.

II

I saw Chaplin in the flesh only once. On 3 September 1972. On the stage of the famous Opera House, *La Fenice*, in Venice's San Marco. The last day of the International Film Festival. At the end of *Il Tutto Chaplin*.

The Opera House was brimming over with people. I was among the lucky ones who had gone to collect their awards, and I had a seat on the stage. Then, accompanied and aided by two officials, that legend of a man walked on to the stage, slowly, with caution. He was eighty-three. It was almost impossible to recognise Charlie. The derby was gone as was the moustache and the tight buttoned-up coat. The stick was nowhere in sight. Not a single trace of his defining persona was present.

He was made to sit there, in the middle of the stage, with two officials on either side. Ailing. His skin wrinkled. I shall never forget that evening. It was a day to remember.

The festival was at Lido, on the Adriatic, the last island in Venice. I watched him there, on the screen, 'a fallen aristocrat at grips with poverty.' He had to tolerate many insults. He knew that 'humiliation is a thing you cannot forget.' His had been a long journey, his experiences varied, and more often than not, amusing. He had faced the world with courage, and often met with defeat. But he had never lost his sense of the humane. With brave Quixotic steps he had almost always moved towards a new horizon.

For those two weeks, all that I had done was rediscover Chaplin and retrace his odyssey. His undaunted progress through troubled times. His unflagging search for man's compassion despite social injustice and political treachery. He was not schooled in politics, but his ear was tuned to the beat of the passing of time.

His reactions were always spontaneous and he never tried to conceal this. *Shoulder Arms* was made in 1918. An unknown Allied soldier (Charlie) arrested the Kaiser. The audience doubled over with laughter. The Kaiser was taken to the nearest camp. And in the very next moment, a line appeared across the screen:

'And peace to the world.' Years later, Chaplin attained a kind of Shavian wit when the murderer of twelve women, Monsieur Verdoux, was being taken to be guillotined (!). He said: 'One murder makes a villain, millions a hero. Numbers sanctify.'

Continuously watching his films for the entire fortnight at Venice, I loved Chaplin, laughed at him, thought about him, and somewhere along the way, I grew wiser. *The Great Dictator* and *Monsieur Verdoux*—these were all logical extension of Chaplin's 'concept of average man' when he crossed the borders of particularity and mimicked the totality of a class—the class that had specialised in genocide. Comical, laughable.

At the end of a long journey that had started in 1914, I finally got to see him that day in the flesh. Everyone in the ancient Opera House went berserk and broke out into deafening applause. And Chaplin was strangely silent that evening. He simply threw a few kisses at the enthralled audience and literally broke down into his chair. My colleagues and I were standing just behind him. The curtain dropped.

III

The next year, at the Tehran Festival, while my wife and I were lunching with the famous French director Rene Clair [1898–1981], one of the luminaries of the twentieth century, we were told that he and his wife had come via Switzerland to meet Chaplin. His condition had deteriorated further, they said. At the lunch table, Clair talked only of Chaplin, and of Oona, Chaplin's fourth wife—the difference of age between the two being embarrassingly wide. He spoke of how she stayed by him constantly. He had to be bathed and dressed and fed. She was an extraordinary woman, and extraordinary was her love.

Chaplin and Geraldine

Whenever the two dictators, Hynkel and Napaloni, met in *The Great Dictator*, Hynkel outsmarted Napaloni in a manner that was hilariously Chaplinesque. Every time it happened, the whole house burst out laughing and the loudest amongst them were the young Italian viewers. I asked a veteran German critic, living in Rome, why young people laughed so hard at the expenses of this one-time national hero. He said: 'For the simple reason that Mussolini lost a war.' His answer made sense to me.

Oona once told an insistent journalist: 'I am married to a young man. People think of Charlie as my father, but age counts for nothing in this house. To me he seems younger every day. There is no father fixation about my feeling for Charlie. He has made me mature and I keep him young ... I never consciously think about Charlie's age for 364 days of the year. Only his birthday is the annual shock for me.'

And Chaplin used to say: 'Oona is my anchor. I needed one, and it is she.'

In 1974, in London, during the release of his book *My Life in Pictures*, Chaplin said that it was not possible for him to take a break because 'ideas just keep popping into my head'. And he added: 'When I go, I go.'

Years continued to roll, and Oona was Chaplin's only companion. He spent hours sitting silently, holding her hand. And referring to Oona as their father's anchor, one of their sons wrote: 'She was able to share that strange solitude of his.'

25 December 1977, Christmas. In the middle of the night, Chaplin died in his sleep.

As he wished, his last rites were performed

unceremoniously. He was buried peacefully in the quiet village, Vevey.

Two months later, the body with the coffin vanished from the grave. Followed a frantic search. The body and coffin were unearthed twenty kilometres away, near Lake Geneva, in a cornfield. The body was finally buried for the second time at the same cemetery in Vevey.

Twenty kilometres away, the farmer and the owner of the cornfield erected a simple wooden cross and, perhaps to mark Chaplin's presence, put a cane on the cross, in memory and tribute.

Chaplin—in a pensive mood 1955

IV

1989, the Centenary of Chaplin. Observed right through the year the world over. But what happened in Cannes at the inaugural presentation of the Annual Festival was an absolute treat. I was there, invited, quietly watching the five-minute event, and I was totally bowled over.

The ambience was splendid, as always. The grand hall was packed to the hilt but not brimming over. There were the luminaries, semi-luminaries, and invitees from all over the world. Not a single seat was empty, not a single person was standing, except, of course, the smiling ushers.

The lights dimmed, the music came on, not too loud, not too low, but made specially for the forty-second edition of the festival—the signature tune.

The curtain was slowly raised and simultaneously the lights in the auditorium were dimmed. The stage revealed a huge cut-out of the eternal tramp Charlie peeping from behind a wall with the five-year old Jackie Coogan, the two trying to outwit the police. It seemed as if they were peering out at all of us, including me, assembled to witness this big event.

Quite often I ask myself—what if Charles Chaplin, during his lifetime, had made a film about the death of his actor (played by himself, as always), buried peacefully only to have it found, after a couple of months, that the coffin was missing—to be discovered after an intense search only to be buried for the second time! My Chaplin, I am pretty certain, would have made a Chaplinesque masterpiece, writing his own obituary.
Just like Saadat Hasan Manto [1912–1955], the great Urdu writer, who, a year before his death, wrote his own epitaph without offering any apology to anyone. He wrote:

Here lies Saadat Hasan Manto.
With him lie buried all the arts and mysteries
of short-story writing.
Under tons of earth he lies,
wondering if he is a greater short-story writer
than God.

I only wish I were the farmer and the owner of the cornfield where the body was hidden by the 'kidnappers'. I would have done exactly what the farmer did. And I would have placed a scarecrow upon the cross, a sweet revenge upon the enemies of men and humanity, in the tradition of 'inspired

Saadat Hasan Manto

nonsense'. And then, borrowing one of his lines, I would have got written on the cross: 'The birds will sing tomorrow.'

Or, perhaps, I would engrave the words he uttered a year before he died: 'To work is to live, and I love to live.'

Or, preferably, I would have carved out a couple of lines from his epitaph, had he deliciously written it in his lifetime.

The cut-out was placed at a significant distance from the proscenium. As the front of the stage lit up, Chaplin's large family was revealed, gathered in front of the footlights. There were about twenty or so of them, all huddled together, some looking normal, some self-conscious and stiff, like a typical nineteenth century photograph of a family group. They were Chaplin's children, some with their spouses, some singles, Chaplin's grandchildren and, maybe, one or two from the next generation as well. Oona Chaplin was missing. Reportedly, she was unwell.

The family looked informal, unusually informal for an occasion like this. A mother breast-feeding her child, a boy scratching his hair, a couple of elders looking a bit stiff, the rest just casual. In the background was the giant of a man, the tramp, father for some and grandfather for others, quietly watching from behind the wall, with the five-year-old Jackie Coogan of *The Kid.*

Geraldine Chaplin, the actor-daughter, took the microphone from its stand and spoke for two minutes or so, touching on the domestic aspects of Chaplin as a father. Before she finished, a child slipped down from his mother's arms and crawled to one end of the stage to pick up the rubber ball which he had probably dropped a little while ago. Ball in hand, he crawled back to be picked up by his mother. Geraldine finished her 'speech' and passed the mike on to one of her brothers. He spoke for not more than half a minute and handed the mike to the next person. Having travelled from hand to hand, the microphone finally reached a small boy, hardly eight or nine, who spoke the shortest line, possibly rehearsed, without knowing what it really meant. Holding the mike close to his mouth, he said: 'I declare the Festival open.'

The enthralled crowd including me witnessed this little show, while, at the same time, the greatest legend of world cinema seemed to watch this domestic scene from behind the wall.

The boy declared the Festival open and instantly the curtain fell, only to rise in a minute, revealing the huge screen. And on the screen appeared the unforgettable scene from *The Great Dictator*—Hynkel's ecstatic game with the 'terrestrial globe', playing savagely, gustily, furiously, with 'the world floating into his hand'. And suddenly, the globe popped.

Cannes 1989 started soon after.

V

Once again, during the Festival in Venice, in the early eighties of the last century, in a luxurious hotel, I had a chance encounter with *Unkown Chaplin.*

Unknown Chaplin, in three parts, compiled and deftly edited by Kevin Brownlow and David Gill. Containing Chaplin's rejected footage from many of his films which, as strictly instructed by him, were never to be used—not even a frame—and all to be destroyed.

Despite his orders, enormous amounts of rushes—shots and sequences—remained dumped without Chaplin's knowledge. Brownlow and Gill used all this, as well as actors and technicians from his time who were still alive and articulate, to make the films. Each was of one hour's duration.

I still remember Jackie Coogan, whom I saw in *The Kid* as a boy and now in *Unknown Chaplin* as a sixty-one-year old, speaking a bit. Remarkable!

Chaplin's new home. Leaving everything in America, his business and his possessions, and preserving his memories—sweet and bitter—Chaplin and Oona came to a quiet village, Vevey, in Switzerland. A three-storeyed house, with gardens all around, a park, a tennis court, spreadout over thirty-seven acres of land. His home. *Manoir de Ban.*

In a neighbouring village, French writer Romain Rolland once lived for a long time. Oona still lives in Vevey, and perhaps still remembers: 'Age counts for nothing.'

Chaplin and his family

This last piece is all about the man, Charles Chaplin, who, for reasons of his own, abandoned the great idea of a sensational project of making a film on Napoleon Bonaparte [1769-1821].

According to David Robinson, the famous researcher and a friend of mine, Chaplin's interest could probably be quite simply explained. While Napoleon offered a uniquely rich role for an actor of small stature, Chaplin was fascinated, so Robinson said, by the character ever since his childhood, when his mother had told him that his father resembled the Emperor. In-between Chaplin's other films, he had kept musing on the project and sat first with a twenty-five-year-old Englishman, Alistaire Cooke; and then, in 1935, with another of the same age, John Strachey [1901-1963], who was already one of the most prominent Left-wing intellectuals in Britain. Chaplin found Strachey fairly amusing and intelligent. The two then developed their ideas for a scenario. The script was completed early in 1936 and was registered as *Napoleon's Return from St. Helena*. Alternative titles suggested were *The Return, The Return from St. Helena, The Return of the Emperor* etc. As usual, the script was polished from time to time; and all done and preserved, it was shelved permanently after about fourteen years. Why it had so remained was unclear, but to the world of films' biggest disappointment, the millions of people could not watch Chaplin as Napoleon.

Comic? Cruel? Thrilling? Funny? Nobody's guess!!!

However, Chaplin did a facial make-up on his own and the dress-maker supplied the costume as instructed by Chaplin. And, reportedly, he looked a satisfying Napoleon Bonaparte—the Emperor!

And that was all. Nothing more. Not even a photograph!

INDEX